A NEW JEWISH ETHICS

A NEW JEWISH ETHICS

S. Daniel Breslauer

Symposium Series

Volume Nine

The Edwin Mellen Press
New York and Toronto

Partial support for the research for this book has been provided by University of Kansas General Research Fund Allocation Grants #3738-20-0038.

BJ
1287
.B783
N49
1983

Library of Congress Cataloging in Publication Data

Breslauer, S. Daniel.
    A new Jewish ethic.
    ISBN 0-88946-700-5

    (Symposium series ; v. 9)
    Includes bibliographical references and index.
    1. Ethics, Jewish. 2. Judaism--20th century.
I. Title. II. Series: Symposium series (Edwin Mellen Press) ; v. 9.
BJ1287.B783N49   1983   296.3'85   83-23659
ISBN 0-88946-700-5

Symposium Series
Series ISBN 0-88946-989-X

Copyright © 1983, S. Daniel Breslauer

All rights reserved. For information contact:

    The Edwin Mellen Press
    P.O. Box 450
    Lewiston, New York 14092

Printed in the United States of America

In Memory of Lynette Myrle Breslauer

February 16, 1913 — May 3, 1981

Table of Contents

Preface: Toward a New Jewish Ethics		1
1.	Judaism as Ecumenical Religion	9
2.	Creation and Process	25
3.	Social Responsibility and Covenant	49
4.	Selfhood and Mitzvah	85
5.	Salvation and Ecumenical Ethics	105
Footnotes		117

PREFACE
TOWARD A NEW JEWISH ETHICS

The Need for a Modern Jewish Ethics

In the past decades American Jews have been forced to face the decisive events of recent history. A haunting question echoes through those decades — what manner of Jewish life is still possible? The question is not whether Jewish life is possible, but how and in what way it is still available. The question arises because when seen through the prism of modern history Judaism appears complicated and Jewish life confused. Since the nineteenth century Jews have chosen diverse and various forms of religious expression. New options for Jewish living have been established. Historical challenges have joined with modern freedom to make Jewish decision-making difficult.

The twin events of the Nazi slaughter of six million Jews and the nearly miraculous creation of the modern State of Israel often serve as symbols of the transformation in modern Jewry. Much modern Jewish thinking takes these two foci as lodestones.[1] Both point to the same reality — Judaism today stands at a crossroad. The Jew must choose whether to affirm this radically altered modern world or to challenge it in the name of traditional values and beliefs. The ethical question which the Jew cannot escape is that of the relationship between modernity and tradition. The moral dilemma for the Jew arises from the inescapability of the contemporary predicament and the equally inescapable demands of an absolute heritage.

The first aspect of this moral challenge is political. Modernity forces a recognition of realistic and harsh political truths. Power rather than ideals, violence rather than peace, propaganda rather than knowledge hold the key to modern political life. The Jew learned this lesson in the Holocaust. Whole sections of humanity can be defined as excess population. Terrorism and racism can be excused as social necessities. Modern history as exemplified in the Holocaust is a Machiavellian teacher. Weakness and vulnerability are fatal flaws.

Modern Israel appears to have learned this lesson well. An isolated and exposed nation in a sea of enemies, Israel has rejected traditional Jewish passivity. In the name of survival, Israeli Jews have taken up the banner of political realism. Pragmatic military goals replace idealisitic hopes; self-interest rather than humanistic values determine how potential enemies are to be treated.

The State of Israel seems a perfect example of Judaism modernized by taking political realism seriously. Jewish survival, however, is more problematic than this conclusion would suggest. Political realism alone is not enough to animate Jewish existence. Jews seek a rationale for their continued survival, a rationale that must be religious rather than merely political.

One reason for this need for spiritual self-justification

is guilt. The survivor of the Holocaust must make sense out of personal existence. How can a person justify surviving when friends and relatives perished? A modern political answer cannot relieve the guilt of survivorship. Only a spiritual answer, a sense of religious purpose can give continued existence a reason for being. A Jewish ethics is needed because although survival depends on political realism, the Jewish person needs a spiritual sense of meaning in order to make that survival worthwhile.

Social ethics is as essential as personal ethics. Whether living in or justifying the State of Israel or defending the right of Jews to form a minority community of their own in a wider culture, the Jew must face social as well as private questions. If Israel is to make claims on Jews throughout the world, it must do so on the basis of a principle higher than nationalism. If Jews are to justify their cultural uniqueness, it must be as a contribution to the broader society. Here again an ethics is needed. While survival may demand that Jews appraise their social and political prospects realistically, *meaningful* survival demands a spiritual justification. The Machiavellian lessons of modern history need to be augmented with religious insight.

Issues in Modern Jewish Ethics

What are the issues raised by modernity? Certainly social and political concerns, particularly those stimulated by modern realism, must make up part of such an ethics. Personal goals and values present another set of problems ethics must address. A more fundamental point, however, needs discussion. Traditionally, the Jew never sought ethical self-justification. Tradition itself *was* ethics. Ethical choosing made little sense in a world where every action was legislated by divine will. The primary ethical issue must be the relevance of Judaism as a source of moral values. Is *Torah*, inherited Jewish teaching, a reliable guide to moral life in the modern world? The moral relevance of *Torah* has been questioned in the modern world. Although the argument is far from settled, many Jews are convinced that it was traditional *Torah* which conditioned Jews to be led like lambs to the slaughter. The modern dilemmas of the State of Israel add another measure of doubt about *Torah*. Moral issues concerning abortion, autopsy, Sabbath observance, war and peace, are often settled by an appeal to pragmatic need rather than *Torah*. Israeli deviation from tradition cannot be condemned out of hand as immoral. Because of the uncertainty with which modern individuals and communities approach ethical standards, *Torah* is no longer an undisputed guide to Jewish behavior. The variety of modern Jewish moral standards is one of the identifying marks of the unique situation confronting the contemporary Jew.[2]

Defining the ethical relevance of *Torah* is the first and most basic issue faced by a modern Jewish ethics. Other concerns flow from this fundamental one. The Jew exists as a member of an identifiable group. Once the moral relevance of Jewish identity is established, questions about social issues must be raised. A modern Jewish ethics will have to be concerned about society and its environment, about social justice, about nationalism and its implications. The ethics of Jewish existence is intrinsically addressed to an individual within a social group. The modern Jew must come to terms with social obligation and its meaning in a Jewish moral life.

The crisis of *Torah* is a complex one. The content of *Torah*, the substance of Jewish ethics, is only one issue involved. Another issue concerns the ideal human life which such an ethic envisions. Jewish law is called in Hebrew *halakhah* — the way or process of human living. The ideal human life is a patterned one; Jewish law is the dynamic struggle to define the shape of that pattern. While Judaism is humanistic in this sense — being focused on human life — it also sees *Torah* as impinging on the divine. *Torah* is an expression of covenant — of the relationship between the divine and the human. The crisis of *Torah* is also a crisis of covenant, a crisis in the modern ability to grasp how human lives can have relevance for the divine. Perhaps "grasp" is the wrong word. The Jew experiences this relevance through the performance of ethical deeds. Legal injunctions are understood as "mitzvot" — acts which bring the human and the divine together. The experience of *mitzvah*, of the partnership between God and human beings, is suspect in the modern world. The crisis of *Torah* is, thus, also a crisis of religious experience. The modern Jew seeks more than a new content to *Torah*; such a Jew searches for a meaningful understanding of *halakhah* — the religious pattern of human living, for a persuasive explanation of covenant —the view that human deeds have divine importance, and for a deepened sense of *mitzvah*, the experiential dimension of ethical living.

Such a Jew finds a bewildering confusion of options in contemporary Judaism. As Eugene Borowitz puts it, "most Jews no longer agree that what Judaism knows best is what God actually wants of us."[3] This skepticism leads to a plethora of alternatives. The variety of answers to the question of what God expects of the Jew is often overwhelming and contradictory.[4]

Some Jews solve this problem pragmatically. They affiliate with an organized Jewish movement and accept the authority of its leader unquestioningly. Liberal Jews follow leaders who emphasize modernity and change tempered by respectful admiration of traditon.[5] Orthodox Jews accept the arbitration of authorized rabbinic interpreters who apply eternal standards to contemporary issues.[6] Conservative Jews are guided by a scholarly class which interprets the dialectic between change and tradition as a means of coping with modernity.[7] Jews who define themselves by affiliation have accepted the meanings of *Torah, halakhah, covenant,* and *mitzvah* established for them by recognized authorities.

The present book advocates a different approach. No authority is taken as decisive; all views, even those of non-Jewish thinkers, are given a hearing. Ethics is understood as a dialogic process of heeding the needs and concerns of others while challenging others on the basis of one's own needs and concerns. *Torah, halakhah, covenant,* and *mitzvah* are conceived not as static but as dynamically evolving from the interchange between Jews and non-Jews and among Jews themselves. Many Jews will disagree with the positions advocated here. The emerging meanings of *Torah, halakhah, covenant,* and *mitzvah* are given as tentative but unsettling challenges to the modern Jew. The logic of an ecumenical ethics demands dialogue as its precondition. I hope that even the disagreement this book arouses will contribute to an open discussion on the issues of personal, social, and religious responsibility. My object is to create a stimulus to that dialogue without which no ethics is possible.

CHAPTER ONE
JUDAISM AS ECUMENICAL RELIGION

Torah as Canon

Torah is the central concept by which Judaism defines itself. If a new Jewish definition develops it must be based on a new meaning given to *Torah*. How are Jews in the modern world to understand themselves and their tradition? The answer given here is as a community in dialogue with other communities. Judaism can be understood as an ecumenical religion. Religious witness to *Torah* affirms intercommunal dialogue. There are Jews who argue against such a view. For them dialogue is unnecessary, even contradictory, to *Torah*. *Torah* implies at best a dialogue between the Jew and God; at worst, a religious monologue.

Torah most literally interpreted, however, is preeminently *canon*, that is the authoritative teachings which define and sustain the Jewish community. If *Torah* as canon implies dialogue and cross-cultural communication, then an ecumenical Judaism can be established. By its very nature canon implies a community for which it functions as a center and foundation. Community unifies diverse individuals through allegiance to a common ideal. Canon creates community by providing that common ideal. Community emerges from individual sacrifice. When individuals, recognizing their interdependence, agree to put aside particularism, share images, institutions, and values, then community is being formed.[1] Canon offers one mechanism for communal formation.

Torah functions in just such a way. Authoritative Jewish teachings enable individuals to come to terms with communal demands. As a source of values transcending social power *Torah* also limits political and social demands upon the individual. *Torah* is ambivalently authoritarian. While demanding individual sacrifice and obedience, it also restricts the arbitrary authority of power groups. As canon, then, *Torah* expands the creative opportunites for both the individual and the society. As a basis for social unity, *Torah* creates the possibility of community action. As a restraint upon political force *Torah* opens personal avenues of self-expression.[2] Canon preserves the tension between individual desire and social order. The creative power of *Torah* emanates from its ability to maintain this tension rather than resolving it by exalting either individual or society.

As canon, then, *Torah* implies at the least a dialogue between the individual and social authority. From its inception, however, Jewish canon has insisted upon a *social* dialogue among competing subcommunities. The biblical context was far from monolithic and in its diversity the meaning of canon as a basis for ecumenical exchange becomes clear. That meaning emerges when prophets like Amos and Hosea hint at an authoritative set of instructions posted in every sanctuary. It becomes even more clear from the early codes and regulations embedded in the biblical corpus. The first fully described canonical community, however, is that established by Josiah's reformation of Judean religion in 621 B.C.E. That reformation demonstrates how an authoritative written word becomes the source of a religious self-understanding.

An interesting dialogue can be found in the pages of the Bible. Two versions of Josiah's reformation are recorded — one in II Kings 22-23 and one in II Chronicles 34-35. Between these two versions there are both similarities and differences. They are in fact a dialogue on ways in which canon can be understood. By looking at the variations involved the ecumenical possibilities of *Torah* can be elucidated. The meaning of canonical community as dialogic religious living emerges from studying these versions of Josiah's reformation.

Judaism as Canonical Community

The two versions tell of King Josiah's reformation of Judean religion. Both agree that the central symbol of this reformation was a book, claimed to be Mosaic revelation. On the basis of this book changes were made in ritual practice, national organization, and religious self-understanding. The event was a community trauma. In its wake leadership roles changed, public witnessing to new social structure, and changed social and political strategies occurred. The communal nature of this trauma was underscored by a national gathering at which public witness and swearing of allegiance were performed.

Canon, as understood by both II Kings and II Chronicles, creates communal loyalty and forms social reality. The nature of both the loyalty required and the society itself is conceived of differently in II Kings and II Chronicles. The former book has the canon initiate religious reform.

Because of the book the land is purged of idols. II Kings lovingly describes the details of that purge, which shrines are destroyed and how the destruction is carried out. For II Chronicles the canon is irrelevant for the destruction of idolatry. The purge precedes the finding of the book. Canon, however, does alter the structure of religious institutions. After it is discovered there is a reorganization of communal worship. New priestly groups are assigned parts in the sacrificial cult. The detailed description involved in II Chronicles focuses on priestly activity.

These differences in view may reflect different historical conditions. Biblical scholars suggest that the author of II Kings responded to pre-exilic needs while the author of II Chronicles was writing in a post-exilic context.[3] Some scholars, however, admit that even in Deuteronomic writing an exilic strand can be detected. This perspective provides a unity between the two versions of Josiah's reformation. The distinctiveness in each version is more theological than historical. Both versions are true representations of that Judaism which is extant even today. Deuteronomic theology, no less than priestly writing, is part of modern Jewish religion. Both represent that tradition of which Jon Levenson has written: "Judaism is the tradition of the synagogue and the yeshivah, not of the Temple, the tradition of prayer and learning rather than of sacrifice."[4] Canonical community consists of this — the exaltation of a book, a scholarly tradition, over the institutions of priest, king, or even prophet. The variations in recording the reformation are diverse strands in a single pattern —the pattern of a community bound together by an authoritative text. Some scholars stress the political divisions which created the diversity within the Canon.[5] Further study, however, will reveal a comprehensive framework into which the diversity can be placed.

"Torah" and Community

The difference between the two renderings of Josiah's story lies in a difference of emphasis. For II Kings the authoritative power of canon is stressed. Community is formed when individuals submit to the abstract authority of an ideal revelation. II Kings stresses the transformed nature of Judean social life. Community depends upon a sacred standard which transcends priest, prophet or king. *Torah* rather than social institutions determines the shape of Judean life. Membership in Jewish religion depends upon a willing acceptance of the jurisdiction of *Torah*. Historical changes may alter external conditions of Jewish life; *Torah* provides a constant and ongoing identity which maintains the community despite historical challenges.

The essential demand of Judaism, according to this emphasis, is obedience to God's ideal standard. A Jew is determined by reference to the unchanging criterion of *Torah*. Many modern Jews affirm this approach to canon. Judaism represents an independent ideal by which Jews judge their lives, by which Jewish identity is authenticated. Samson Raphael Hirsch echoes this view and claims: "Only by devoting all our activities, all our existence and wishes, to the guidance by divine laws" can Jews live authentically. He extends this idea from the personal sphere to the social arena: "Just as this obedience is the sole condition for our lives as individuals, so does it set the same task for our *national* life."[6]

This view reinforces the belief that Jewish community depends upon adherence to a transcendent standard. Just as Josiah's reformation, as portrayed in II Kings, sees all religious authenticity flowing from the finding of the Mosaic canon, so Hirsch sees true religious community in obedience to revelation. The mark of *kehillah*, Jewish community, is fidelity to *Torah*. Only when the details of revelation are put into practice can a Jewish community be born. Without unconditional adherence to *Torah* religious life is impossible.[7]

The view in II Kings suggests the *Torah* comes first and only then is community formed. In II Chronicles Josiah has created authentic community before finding the Mosaic revelation. Josiah has restructured Judah's religion, but only in a preliminary way. Josiah expresses the fundamental religious insight — God makes demands on society; human beings must change their ways. Josiah's instincts are true; he provides a living religious center around which community can flourish.

True community, however, is expressive as well as obediental. Josiah removed the obstacles to religious expression before finding the Mosaic code. He then used that code to create an expressive religious cult. This is a second way in which *Torah* supports community. *Torah* can be a tool whereby communal religious expression is made possible. Canon understood this way is secondary to community. Religious life provides a framework within which new experience is possible. When Josiah reconstitutes Jewish community he begins with internal religious orientation; he then provides through canon a new symbolism and ritual system to express that orientation.

If *Torah* is expressive rather than formative, does it express a specific content? Perhaps the community itself may be said to be its content. Jewish religious community develops through historical experience. A sense of this dynamic process of religious growth is conveyed by the story of the Josianic reformation and its consequences. Not content but religious self-examination is primary.

JUDAISM AS ECUMENICAL RELIGION

Different contents may be equally Canon if continuing the identical encounter with the divine. Thus, the meaning of Judaism is found in process. Martin Buber describes the Bible in just such a way. It records "the encounter between a group of people and the Lord of the world in the course of history."[8] Community is prior and *Torah* is to be judged as an authentic or inauthentic reflection of the events forming communal identity.

This view of *Torah* contrasts with that of the authoritarian emphasis. There the question was an individual's authenticity. Here the question is the authenticity of the tradition. The ethical problem at stake in determining Jewish religion is that of balancing personal authenticity and social authority. Each Jew is caught between two demands — that of challenging the self in the name of an ideal tradition and that of challenging the tradition in the name of a realized and vital communal reality. Again Martin Buber's insight is helpful. He declared that "world history is the battle between false and genuine authority; each man of faith is obliged to take part in this battle."[9] Belief in *Torah* is ethical only if the struggle between genuine and inauthentic authority is mirrored in the believer.

"Torah" as Ecumenical

The Bible as presently constituted emphasizes both tests of authenticity. The individual must submit to canonical authority; the canon must express true religious life. Our present text is intentionally ambivalent. As Joseph Blenkinsopp points out: "The canon, then, does not lend itself to a definitive solution of the problem of religious authority . . . [but] suggests rather than unresolved tension, an unstable equilibrium."[10] This intentional ambiguity reflects an ecumenical openness to differing approaches to the meaning of Jewish life.

Gershom Scholem, explaining the way in which Jewish mystics interpreted the multilayered meanings of *Torah*, commented on what he called "the unlimited mystical plasticity of the divine word." He suggested that such a flexible approach to canonical teachings "is perhaps the only way in which the idea of a revealed word of God can be taken seriously."[11] Certainly the mystics demonstrate how Judaism can develop through ecumenical dialogue. For the mystical interpreter of *Torah* four levels of meaning appear in every text. On one level, the authoritative injunctions to specific actions must be taken seriously and literally. *Torah* forms community by defining correct and inappropriate actions. On other levels, however, *Torah* indicates an allegorical, sermonic, or mystic meaning.[12] Personal experience and the reality of lived social experience are useful measures of *Torah*. The truth of Judaism is as much experiential as authoritarian. A dialogue between life and text, between inherited values and historical demands is part of *Torah* itself.

This dialogue occurs in history — a history which includes non-Jews as well as Jews. The Jewish mystic lived in a Christian environment; even the multilayered understanding of holy scripture may have been influenced by that environment . Christian piety exercised some influence on Jewish pietism. *Torah* demands ecumenical religion because the perspective of history is shaped by forces external to Judaism. A clear-sighted understanding of *Torah* requires both the faithful witness to historical authority of tradition and the sensitive awareness of contemporary meaning which ecumenical discussion with non-Jews brings. The *Torah* transforms Judaism from a parochial into an ecumenical community.

JUDAISM AS ECUMENICAL RELIGION

Because of *Torah* the Jew remains distinctive in the world refusing to abandon cultural identity.

The Bible and Ecumenism

An ecumenical Judaism is one that understands itself both as bound to authority and responsive to modern challenges. Such a Judaism looks to non-Jews no less than to other Jews to discover the direction in which Jewish life should grow. Together with many Christians, Jews who accept this ecumenical perspective will see biblical authority less in terms of unchanging details but in terms of a community of faith. Perhaps a better expression would be communities of faith. An ecumenical approach to Judaism will admit that the biblical canon has created not one but many religious communities. As James Barr points out, the Bible from its very inception refused to restrict the concept of "people of God" to only one believing community. The network of images and meanings within the Bible stimulated a plurality of communities, each of which accepted the same canon as its center.[13]

This understanding of the Bible is the preconditon for meaningful dialogue between Jews and Christians. As Monika Hellwig suggests, "A meaningful dialogue can begin when the Bible is recognized not as a literal account of what happened, but as a collection of interpretations of what happened."[14] An ecumenical Judaism can enter the discussion of biblical authority with frankness, willing to risk hearing the Bible differently in a different context. Such a Jew will also affirm the canon as formative and remain distinguishable from the Christian, thereby being able to contribute distinctively to dialogue.

This element of undissoluble distinctiveness is part of

the canonical heritage. Canon forms community no less than it expresses it. Christians can understand this approach. John Bright captures this recognition when he decides that the canon "must be closed." As a narrative of "saving history," of "Heilsgeschichte," the Bible gives witness that at a certain time in a certain place certain specific actions took place which transformed all history. Only a discrete account of particular events can provide such salvation history. Community draws its life from those events and no others. Communal life depends upon having a closed canon, a set of definitive events associated with the beginnings of community itself.[15] An ecumenical sharing of biblical insight will include a candid recogniton that Jews and Christians do not, in fact, trace themselves to the same formative history. The same book provides different crucial events of salvation history for each community. It is in the name of these events that the communities are distinct and separate from each other. The first moral demand of a modern Jewish ethics is that it maintain Jewish loyalty to the formative definition of Judaism. A second moral imperative is that it be flexible enough to respond to the changed realities of Jewish life in a transformed world, a world of ecumenical dialogue. The authenticity of any Jewish answer must face a twofold test: that of the tradition and that of contemporary life. Both tests are administered in the process of dialogue with Jews and non-Jews.

The Institutional Ethics of an Ecumenical Judaism

Jewish authenticity may be tested in ecumenical dialogue; Jewish existence demands that those tests be institutional as well as personal or ideological. Authentic Judaism is lived and experienced through communal institutions. An ecumenical Judaism must authenticate

JUDAISM AS ECUMENICAL RELIGION

its institutions as well as the content of its Jewish religiousness. The test, of course, lies in the openness of institutions to dialogue with others. Both Judaism and Christianity share the biblical legacy of open institutions.[16] The dynamics of the Josianic reformation show how institutions evolve in response to religious innovation. An ecumenical Judaism will make that responsive evolution a criterion for institutional authenticity.

Certainly such an approach entails risks. A traditionalist would insist that Judaism has no need for dialogue or ecumenical openness. The ecumenical Jew admits that no single institution is sufficient in itself, that the tradition alone may be inadequate for a full human life, that religious meaning may be deepened by contact with religious traditions other than ones own. John T. Pawilkowski enters ecumenical dialogue with such an admission. He calls on Christians to recognize that "Christianity in and by itself does not contain in their fullness all the insights or experiences necessary for a complete understanding of the religious dimension of the human person."[17] The ecumenical Jew is called upon to do likewise. Jewish institutions are to risk their claims to absolute authority, their relegation of opposing views to inauthenticity. An ecumenical ethics of Judaism will be an ethics of risk. Institutions must risk their power in order to meet the test of an ecumenical Judiasm.

A new Jewish ethics is revolutionary not only because it challenges tradition in the name of new historical situations. Jews in the past looked at *Torah* through the lenses of their contexts. Ecumenical Judaism is revolutionary because it demands institutional flexibility. It addresses the power centers of Jewish life and calls upon them to limit their control. Jewish institutions are to become servants of the ecumenical idea rather than masters of Jewish life.

Although revolutionary such a view is not unprecedented. Josiah's reformation issued just such a call. The institutions of priest, king, and prophet were subordinated to *Torah* by that reformation. As an ambivalent, emerging religious perspective *Torah* required flexibility and change from Jewish institutions. Ecumenical Judaism today renews Josiah's call. *Torah* as an ecumenical reality must have priority over either traditionalist authority or communal necessity. The ethical task must address institutions and include them in dialogue; institutional openness to religious exchange must be cultivated. An ecumenical Judaism creates a social ethics of change and growth.

Ecumenical Judaism and the Ethics of Belief

Ecumenical Judaism requires the individual to submit to authority and authority to submit to scrutiny. It addresses institutions no less than individuals. Ecumenical *Torah* also implies a specifically religious task — believing in God's commanding presence. Will Herberg has claimed that "Revelation is of the past, but it has no meaning unless and until it becomes existentially operative in the contemporaneous present."[18] This means that the individual is responsible for making belief in a received tradition a vital reality of the present. The ethics of an ecumenical Judaism insists that belief is authenticated only in the conflict and tension of interpersonal dialogue.

Authentic and genuine belief must meet the ecumenical test. Beliefs which shun the realities of human experience, that avoid conflict, that refuse to admit challenges, that hide behind dogmas fail to confront experience honestly. An ecumenical Judaism demands the honesty of belief tried in the tensions of everyday life. Some of these tensions arise from the modern social situation. Others are products of internal, personal confusion. An ecumenical Judaism will reject the escapism which blockades doubts. *Torah* depends on challenge as well as upon acceptance and authority. Belief in *Torah* is honest only if won through an engagement with life's realities.

Ecumenical Judaism and Moral Decision

What is Judaism? The sketch above suggests that *Torah* by its very nature avoids answering that question. Judaism is *Torah* as understood within a particular community. One such community is that of ecumenical Judaism which sees *Torah* developing through interaction, with both internal and external dialogue directing that development. On the basis of an ecumenical Judaism a Jew can begin facing the major moral decision modernity demands. The issues of modern life — science and the human control of nature, society, nationalism and political ethics; personal life, sexuality, and private destiny — can be addressed using the criteria of an ecumenical ethics.

The first requirement of this ethics is a rigorous examination for authenticity. Two elements comprise this examination — an honest look at the modern situation and a faithful attention to Jewish tradition. Neither element has the final say. The decisive ethical fact will be the conflict, the tension, the creative balance between them. Tradition must be challenged by the realistic situation and its needs. The validity of those needs must be evaluated in the light of the tradition and through the demands which that tradition makes.

The second criterion of an ecumenical Jewish ethics is that of institutional responsiveness. Moral questions of social and political responsibility must be raised. An ecumenical Jewish ethics must take account of how institutions are involved and what their moral obligations are. Each moral decision has a social dimension that must be considered. An ecumenical Jewish ethics will look at that social dimension in terms of the open institutions of Jewish life.

Finally the ethics of belief must be raised. The persuasiveness of a particular moral stand for the individual is a crucial ethical test. An ecumenical ethics must raise the relevance of a moral decision for personal self-understanding. The honesty of that decision as an expression of personality must be examined.

The goal here is to sketch the problems in moral life facing the modern Jew. The ecumenical perspective provides a vantage point from which these issues can be studied. The approach advocated here does not choose between solutions as such but suggests how they combine together and how an ecumenical perspective can understand them. Perhaps the most important contribution these sketches offer is an affirmative view of conflict and a belief that from tension can come creative religious life.

CHAPTER TWO
CREATION AND PROCESS: HALAKHAH AND THE NATURAL ORDER

The Vulnerability of Nature and Halakhic Crisis

The most monumental crisis facing the modern Jew is only superficially a matter of social ethics. Deciding how far human control over nature should extend, confronting the dilemma of human destructive power, is more than a moral challenge to social institutions. Human destructiveness may not be new; the ability to alter the very structure of nature, however, is a modern marvel. The moral question raised by that ability extends beyond ordinary social ethics.[1] Human beings have learned to mold nature in their own image, and that image is often an ambiguous one. Human artifice has transformed the processes of procreation, birth, sexual development, and death. Natural events that seemed inevitable, unalterable, and unshakeable have been disrupted by modern science. Nature itself now seems to share the "treacherous impurity of everything human."[2] Modernity poses a peculiar moral problem: Given the ability of human beings to restructure nature, is an independent standard for human creativity possible? What moral limits can be established for human interference in the natural world? Both natural law and human nature are vulnerable to new definitions. The value and purpose of human experimentation with the world has become a problem as human power continues to increase. Since nature is apparently a human creation there seems little guidance from the natural world to aid in deciding how human beings should deal with their newly discovered abilities.

The problems raised by this question vary in their immediate application to personal life. Some questions are social and political — examples being, how responsible is a society for its environment, what obligations fall upon nations possessing nuclear weapons, how much control over genetic and physical life does a society possess. Other questions arise in times of physical crisis —for example, what criteria determine true "death," can "living" organs from a "dead" person be given to a desperate patient, how is a woman to respond to an unwanted pregnancy. Still other questions require moral reflection of a more permanent nature — for example, what are the limits and uses of experimentation on human beings, what is the relationship between a society's need for certain physical and psychological traits and personal decision-making. These problems arise because nature is vulnerable to human interference; nature can be molded and shaped by human intention.

One response to this problem gives the individual absolute power. Decisions about genetic engineering, organ transplants, abortion, euthanasia, or even social responsibility are private and personal. In contrast to that self-directed approach, ethicists insist on the need for an external standard of right and wrong. The individual so

CREATION AND PROCESS

often makes decisions on the basis of spontaneous feelings rather than informed understanding that personal response is rightly suspected. Even public consensus is easily swayed by emotional rather than factual arguments. As one Jewish writer notes, "Moral questions of such gravity cannot be resolved simply by reference to the fickle whims of the individual conscience or of public opinion."[3] Some ideal or value outside of the individual is needed to guide decision-making.

The first test for a Jewish morality of science is its authenticity within Judaic traditon. That tradition has never denied that human beings have power, that they can create as well as destroy. The vulnerability of nature was recognized just as the potential of humanity for partnership in nature's creativity. God gave nature its shape and meaning, but authorized human acitivity as an essential part of the divine plan. Human power, however, is restricted to the boundaries given by God's blueprint. Humanity can "change, produce, and create," but it has no right to "repeal" the basic laws of nature.[4] God's creativity is the source of human creative strength; human action which acknowledges divine creation is productive; human striving against the created purposes of the world is destructive.

Creation and Sabbath

Creation, then, is the key to a Jewish ethics of science. Scientific power, technological innovation, medical discoveries are to be tested against the ideals inherent in God's creative action. When Jews weigh their response to modern issues in bio-ethics they do so with full awareness of a divine design comprehending all creation. The importance of creation as a theological principle cannot be emphasized too much. It is the cornerstone of Jewish belief and from it stem other elements in Jewish faith including affirmation of *Torah*, trust in miracles, and Israel's chosen destiny.[5]

Belief in creation points to a certain attitude by which the Jew is oriented towards nature and human responsibility. This belief depends fundamentally on a way of looking at the world. The world is not haphazard or accidental. The forces within nature are not arbitrary, but planned and purposeful. Whether creation took the form described in Genesis is less important than the affirmation that God, not chance, determines the shape of reality. The theological meaning of creation lies in this acceptance of a divine order. Because God is creator, human actions in the created world must be tempered to meet the requirements of the divine design.[6]

Sabbath observance provides a practical and concrete expression of the theology of creation. Sabbath rest reminds the Jew of God's creative power. Even if the biblical story is only a symbol of divine creativity, a weekly celebration of that creativity is important. During the Sabbath a Jew acknowledges that God's will, not human desire, sets the framework for human creativity. By obeying Sabbath law the Jew restrains wanton impulses in the name of higher values.

Sabbath worship and ritual, however, celebrate human power no less than human obedience. The Sabbath is a reminder of the exodus from Egypt as well as of the creation of the world. On the Sabbath the Jew recalls that freedom is a divine gift. Human creativity is a precious possession — but it is granted by the creator and not an absolute possession. When Jews follow Sabbath law they proclaim three beliefs — that God has created a good world, that human creativity can hallow that world, and

CREATION AND PROCESS

that obedience is a proper response of the creature to the creator. A traditionalist Jew would insist that these ideas are fully expressed only when all the laws of Sabbath observance are followed. Without the humility of obedience the creature has not truly understood the power of the creator. The purpose of Sabbath obedience is to demonstrate that a Jew "uses his skills not as of right, but by permission of the Creator."[7] The *mitzvoth*, the particular commandments associated with the Sabbath, are part of a greater whole. That whole is *Halakhah*, the way of Jewish existence. For *Halakhah*, to be is to obey. Life is most natural when in conformity with divine design.

Obedience alone seems rather legalistic. It seems as if abiding by the law were a value by itself. The Jew obeys God's law because that law leads to self-fulfillment. On the Sabbath the Jew refrains from interfering with nature because of a deep trust that nature is God's, and being God's is good. By following Sabbath law a Jew demonstrates confidence in divine wisdom; trust that even without human intervention the natural order can flourish.[8]

But human beings do intervene in the world process. Human actions lend a dimension to experience that nature alone cannot achieve — the dimension of holiness. Creation is a preparation. By acknowledging that preparation the Jew can move to fulfillment. The Sabbath is to be sanctified, to be made holy. Through worship and study, through rituals and dedication, the Sabbath is transformed into an experience beyond time and space. The Sabbath shows wherein human beings exceed nature. As Martin Buber suggests, "The meaning with which Creation informed man, informed the world, is fulfilled through the hallowing."[9] *Halakhah* is not only a way of obedience, of trust in the divine, but also a way of confidence in human holiness.

The Process of Creation: An Ecumenical Halakhah

A modern Jewish ethics must meet the test of tradition. No Jewish morality is possible which does not take creation seriously. Yet an ecumenical morality must take the challenges of modernity seriously as well. Humility, trust in God, and confidence in humanity have been transformed by contemporary life and experience. Humility must now face the awesome power of human science. Obedience to received laws is justified when those laws address the real situation in which people live. The symbolic meaning of Sabbath restrictions on fire seem stretched beyond recogniton when applied to automobiles and electric lights. Fetal research makes ancient ways of understanding the unborn strangely inappropriate. A modern Jewish ethics must approach the received tradition cautiously. Just as the Jew is humble before God, so modern science should elicit a new humility. An appreciation of the changed cosmos, of the new natural world in which human beings live and which they created will stimulate a revised view of obedience. God's laws as revealed in science may mean a new understanding of Jewish obligaton to the Creator.

Trust in God requires a different sort of response in the age of nuclear power than in earlier ages. The realization that human beings are not mere passive recipients of nature but participate in shaping it means that the ideal of letting the cosmos act independently is hardly realizable. Human interference in natural order is impossible to halt. Even Sabbath regulations do not in fact prevent Jewish homes from using air conditioners, plastics, chemicals and other pollutants. A modern Jewish ethics must face the cruel fact that human beings have made even nature demonic. A naive trust in cosmic order is deluding. A

CREATION AND PROCESS

modern *Halakhah* cannot continue to construe natural phenomenon as unambivalent expressions of divine order. The way of the world now is such that a dialogue between ideal Jewish visions of nature's articulation of God's plan and the dark reality that exists is no longer possible. An ethics which refuses to admit the transformed shape of nature has failed to provide adequate moral guidance in the modern world.

A *Halakhah* which emphasizes the human role of sanctification of creation cannot escape the modern reality of human desecration. Often this desecration occurs unwittingly. Tradition itself may instill those values of exploitation and manipulation that transforms nature from a divine responsibility into a victim. A ritualism which reflects only inward on itself can scarcely find its own faults. Dialogue with other traditions is a safeguard against that desecration which arises from a perversion of ideals. The human task of cultivating nature can easily become license to exploit it. Together with a ritualistic sanctification of the world, a new *Halakhah* would require ecumenical exchange. Through that exchange Jews and non-Jews would challenge one another. Although the ideals both share would be constant the challenges would prevent sanctification from becoming, through misuse, desecration. A modern Jewish ethic would seek an ecumenical *Halakhah* arising from a dialogue between the theological meaning of creation and the harsh realityies of modern experience.

This ecumenical *Halakhah* is based on two principles. In the first place it affirms traditional insight. Human beings need the restraint of divine guidance. The world is not humanity's playground but a created environment for a divine plan. Human beings are important participants in the world but the natural order has a strong and beneficent impulse of its own. The essential human task is that of hallowing nature, of freely cultivating the divine potential of existence. Secondly, however, the new *Halakhah* admits that modernity brings special problems which require different responses — often unanticipated in the tradition. The unprecedented power of human science means that traditional laws must be refashioned; the awsome possibility of transforming nature means a new sensitivity to ways in which human understanding of nature may be misguided; the ambiguity of sanctification urges caution in a simple acceptance of all values inherited from an earlier time.

The essential point of this ecumenical *Halakhah* is that of process. The relationship between human beings and their environment is a changing, growing one. As that relationship becomes more complex, so the ethics governing it must be more complex. An ecumenical *Halakhah* directs this growth to new complexity through dialogue — dialogue between tradition and modernity, dialogue between differing religious traditions. As Jews wrestle with modern questions they must do so fully aware of the ambiguities involved and the tension between an inherited value system representing an ideal divine expectation.

Creation and Society: Institutional Obligations

Questions raised by modern science have social implications. Society has a stake in discoveries which transforms the life of its members. *Halakhah* cannot remain a parochial concern of some individuals, or even of an isolated religious community. The ecumenical demand for self-criticism through exposure to other views already moves *Halakhah* into the social sphere.

An ecumenical *Halakhah* requires open institutions that are flexible enough to respond to new possibilities in the natural world. Without open institutions the challenges which keep ideals from becoming tools of desecration are suppressed. The institutional implication of such an emphasis on dialogue is the refusal to allow any dogmatism an absolute authority. Of course, societies have military priorities; of course, they have an interest in the birth rate and health of their members. An ecumenical ethics, however, declares immoral any society which establishes one and only one legitimate response to a medical, scientific, or environmental question. While a society may legislate certain decisions — regarding, for example, autopsies, nuclear weapons, contraception, or genetic engineering — such legislation is illegitimate if it claims to do more than provide pragmatic and *limited* order. A society which seeks to answer questions of life and death, sexuality, and environmental concerns from a definitive and absolute position has usurped the rights of its subcommunities. An ecumenical *Halakhah* cannot be content with social legislation that happens to agree with a traditional point of view. It must rather protect that ongoing dialogue which alone prevents the subversion of ideals for selfish and short-sighted interests.

Creation and the Individual: Toward a Psychology of Creation

Creation, as noted above, is an attitude towards the world and the self, not belief in a literal narrative. Even understood in this way, however, creation is a difficult idea to affirm. Modern individuals often experience the world as a chaotic challenge. Life seems out of control; the self seems barraged by hostile forces. If an ecumenical *Halakhah* sees creation as essential, can it be an honest reflection of the modern experience?

Traditional Judaism offers each individual a series of opportunities for affirming creation. Study and prayer, Sabbath observance and personal obedience to divine precepts reinforce a sense of meaning and order. The ecumenical Jew moves outside of the safe confines of these traditional rituals. The honesty of an ecumenical *Halakhah* comes when new experiences — of frustration and failure no less than of success and security — are incorporated into Jewish life. An ecumenical *Halakhah* will use the symbols of human concern as the basis for acknowledging creation. Abortion no less than birth can be an expression of the divine will. Nuclear experimentation as well as kindling a fire is an abomination and desecration of the Sabbath.

The challenge of an ecumenical *Halakhah* is that of making the biblical insight that God "creates light and darkness, ordains good and evil" a concretely real experience. Creation is not a concept which *explains* modern life; it solves no problems. Instead it symbolizes the problem. If human beings had no sense of purpose, then modern chaos would not be disturbing. By giving expression to human frustration and sense of conflict, an ecumenical *Halakhah* gives creation a modern meaning which helps an individual confront the realities of life.

Abortion: A Useful Example

An ecumenical ethics can be applied to the various moral issues involved in a person's relationship to nature. Questions of medical experimentation, for example, are hotly debated by Jews.[10] Sexual morality involves another set of controversial issues.[11] The basic concern, however, is one of authority — what authority does the tradition have to determine how an individual acts and what authority do social bodies have to legislate behavior. The

CREATION AND PROCESS

problems involved in such debates can be illustrated by looking at one example — that of abortion and its consequences in the modern situation.

One major problem the modern Jew faces is that of defining abortion. Whereas Jewish tradition makes a distinction between a viable fetus and one not yet viable, modern science challenges such a view. Judaism seeks to protect the mother from harm, but modern views of "harm" are so extensive that the question of when an abortion is required to save the mother and when it is merely "on demand" is very difficult to answer. While Judaism seems to legitimate some type of abortion, defining that type is more difficult than it might appear.

A second problem is that of government intervention. Jews have sometimes allowed social legislation to override permissive Jewish tradition — the case of monogamy is one example of where Jewish permissiveness gave way to social custom. The good of the entire society might require legislation which particular Jews might deem unsatisfacory. The exact role of civil government in determining whether abortions should or should not be permitted requires discussion and examination.

A third question to be raised is that of the effect of abortion on an individual woman. That effect is hardly unambiguous. While for many women the trauma of an unwanted pregnancy justifies an abortion, for others it does not. How a woman regards herself, what she sees as her primary life function, how she justifies her sexuality are important aspects of her reaction to the question of abortion. Any attempt to solve the issue of abortion without recognizing the variety of responses made by different women is clearly distorted. The crisis of abortion for the individual cannot be summarized in any general statement. Personal reaction is as crucial here as in any other human sphere. A morality addressing the question of abortion must confront this element of personal individuality.

An Ecumenical Discussion of Abortion

A Jew wrestling with the morality of abortion often finds traditional answers ambivalent. What actually is the standard of a traditionalist? Certainly traditional authorities differ among themselves — sometimes even a single authority will change his view as to whether a particular type of fetus is to be aborted.[12] When is the fetus viable? Although most Jewish scholars suggest that during the first trimester the fetus is "only water," there is a dissenting view. J. David Bleich admits that "the status of an embryo's claim to life during the first forty days following conception is not entirely clear."[13] The specific details of Jewish morality concerning abortion are often confusing.

The basic principle, however, is fairly clear — the tradition turns to precedent and *halakhic* methods in order to solve the questions surrounding abortion. An ecumenical ethics must take this principle as the test of a Jewish morality. An individual who refuses to submit to the scrutiny of inherited *halakhic* precedent, has forfeited Jewish authenticity. The answers given by that precedent, however, are as noted, often far from clear. A willingness to expose oneself to accumulated Jewish precedent does not preclude personal response and individual differences.

One area in which those differences are clear is in the Jewish concern for the welfare of the mother. No Jewish

CREATION AND PROCESS

scholar opposes an abortion when the mother's life is in danger. An ecumenical ethics, however, recognizes that deciding when life is in danger is often difficult. An interplay of precedent and personal uniqueness is needed in order to make any particular decision. The unique aspects of any specific situation mean that a variety of options do, in fact, exist. The literature concerning the principle of danger to the mother demonstrates the ambiguity of the ideal at stake.[14] Certainly no decision can be made unilaterally. A doctor alone does not know the entire psychological impact of an abortion on a particular woman. The woman herself may be subject to intense stress and later regret a decision made in the heat of the moment. No one source can definitively decide whether a particular pregnancy is actually of severe danger to the mother.[15] The need for ecumenical discussion, for allowing a dialogue between traditional values and the various concrete elements of any particular circumstance, is crucial if the goals of tradition itself are to be attained.

One of the most vocal groups opposing an authoritarian Jewish tradition is that of Jewish feminism. Feminists criticize the *halakhic* structure which imposes a system devised by a male elite upon women. Certainly an ecumenical ethics would decry any morality which excludes the moral agent from the decision-making process. If women cannot participate in forming that *halakhah* which shapes their destinies, then they have been denied a life moral option. A Jewish morality created by men for women is a moral scandal. Although men in the rabbinic tradition have been sensitive to women, have sought to alleviate their condition, and have responded to women's needs, they have not included women in the mainstream of *halakhic* creativity. An ecumenical ethics demands that the question of abortion be discussed by women no less than by men.

At the same time the authenticity of this morality as a *Jewish* morality must give binding power to inherited precedent — even though that precedent has been created by an exclusively male elite. Any morality demands self-limitation, restricts the possibilities of a person's actions. An ecumenical ethics sees in the abortion issue an opportunity for dialogue between women, now conscious in a more vital way than ever before of their needs, rights, and potential, and Judaic precedent, now as always, expressing certain unchanging ideals, standing beyond changing historical contingencies, shaping human life in a distinctive way. Blu Greenberg proposes just such a dialogue. She urges that Jewish women take traditional *Halakhah* seriously while demanding that the *Halakhah* be flexible enough to respond to genuine feminist complaints. She argues that "stressing a woman's right to control her own body . . . should go hand in hand with emphasis on the sanctity of life."[16] Jewish women should demonstrate that their Jewishly informed affirmation of life and moral obedience to divine precept can be compatible with moral choice and a sensitive recognition of the positive as well as negative elements in abortion. Abortion is a multifaceted option. Jewish precedent can illuminate some aspects of that option; personal response by individual women can illuminate still other aspects. Ecumenical discussion provides a context for moral decisions. Without such discussion a woman would submit to an external authority; her response to an unwanted pregnancy would cease to demonstrate moral sensitivity and be merely a conditioned acceptance of a

CREATION AND PROCESS

male standard. Were she not to take traditional precedent seriously a woman would also forfeit her moral worth. By following personal inclination without a vigorous examination of it by applying an independent measure, she has evaded her moral responsibility. Only an ecumenical interaction between tradition and personal self-assertion can lead to genuine moral decision.

In the process of reaching those decisions both women and tradition are transformed. If the meaning of *Halakhah* refers to the process of existence, then tradition must risk undergoing transformation in that process and women risk being changed as well. In confronting abortion as an ambiguous possibility a woman with an unwanted pregnancy is a force for growth in Jewish religion even as Jewish religion helps her grow.

Social Institutions and Abortion: An Ecumenical Suggestion

The Jewish individual struggles with the authenticity of a moral response to the question of abortion. When might an abortion meet the demands of traditional morality? When might moral considerations for a particular woman mean that the tradition itself must change? An ecumenical ethics realizes that any discussion of abortion must also face the challenge of institutional power. Does any social or political institution have the moral right to impose its decisions about abortion on the population as a whole? Perhaps society should remain neutral in this case. Women should have the right to decide for themselves what moral obligations they have to an unborn fetus. An alternative argument would stress the social implications of any and every birth. Society may need to stimulate a growing birth rate; it may need to discourage certain types of births. Perhaps abortion is a legitimate social concern and as such institutional pressure is not only a helpful resource for civil government but a moral responsibility.

Jewish thinkers are divided on this issue. Balfour Brickner feels that religious groups have inserted abortion into power politics illegitimately. American life, he claims, is based on respect for individual liberty, on the right to free choice. Religious dogmas may persuade some members of society; they should not legislate the common behavior of all citizens.[17] An opposing view takes the position that society has an obligation to protect its citizens. Just as society can legislate against murder, so too it can legislate against misuse of a fetus. Even if Jewish law opposes regarding a fetus as a full human life, it recognizes the right of a civil government to define murder in its own way. Seymour Siegel defends those who seek to abolish all abortion as exercising their "constitutional right." No Jew should oppose such a genuine expression of social conscience.[18]

An ecumenical *Halakhah* would not brand every attempt to legislate behavior about abortion as immoral. The morality of such legislation, however, would lie less in its expression of religious values than in its pragmatic effect upon the social situation. Certainly no ecumenical ethics could approve of social legislation which would make one religious institution supreme. Attempting to legislate the particular morality of a specific religious group would close off avenues of dialogue and intergroup discussion. Yet an ecumenical ethics would encourage discussion of the social needs served by legislation of abortion. A society does have a legitimate interest in the procreative processes of its citizens. It also has a responsibility of protecting personal freedom and privacy. Legislation concerning abortion is moral only if it balances these two responsibilities.

Ecumenical ethics sees a public, civil discussion of abortion appropriate only if within certain guidelines. Civil leaders should judge abortion on the basis of social not religious considerations. The focus of the moral issue is not that of either the fetus or the mother but rather the relationship between a government and individuals. A government demonstrates its humility by recognizing where and when it should not intervene in private lives. Individuals display their trust of government and recognition of social obligation by acceding to demands that may affect their sexual lives. The morality of social legislation concerning abortion has two elements — the moral sensitivity of social leaders to the private space needed by individuals and the moral strength of citizens who recognize legitimate claims made by civil government upon its citizens.

Abortion and the Individual: Personality in Crisis

How persuasive is an ecumenical ethics for an individual struggling with the crisis of unwanted pregnancy? A traditional morality provides a sense of relief, escape from traumatic decision making. An entirely subjective morality strengthens self-confidence and liberates a woman from false priorities. An ecumenical morality, however, demands an honest acceptance of trauma and conflict. From such a morality a woman learns not to expect easy answers, not to be confused or dismayed by her own ambivalence. The advantage of an ecumenical approach to morality is that it cultivates self-acceptance.

The Jewish woman finds unwanted pregnancy a moral problem just because she affirms a complex value system. Judaism depends upon family life to provide continuity throughout generations. Without political structures to secure continued Jewish identity traditional Judaism transformed the family into the major socializing agent. The Jewish theologian Seymour Siegel echoes Jewish concerns when he looks ambivalently on women's liberation. He celebrates the new found freedom, but he also fears it. "The liberation of the woman and the opportunities which should be hers to fulfill her intellectual and spiritual needs," he comments, "should not be achieved at the price of removing the woman from her vital function within the family structure."[19] Many Jewish women accept this statement. They, too, are frightened by the implications of too much freedom.

The values of modernity, however, have taught many women to challenge accepted Jewish norms. The single woman has been defined as incomplete, as less than fully realized. If woman's primary function is familial, then a single woman has no chance to actualize her potential. Jewish women are reclaiming the possibility of a fulfilled single life.[20] Sacrificing the role of childbearer may be a liberation by which a woman becomes more fully human. While the implications of Judaism cannot be ignored, they can and often are challenged. Even when they struggle for a new self-definition Jewish women still seek to be recognized as Jews.

The question of an unwanted pregnancy raises the issues of woman's role in a peculiarly acute way. The tension between a traditional affirmation of woman's familial obligations and her duties towards herself is revealed in the crisis of deciding about abortion. An easy solution which accepts either tradition's dictums or the desires of the self has been false to the complexity of the situation. An ecumenical ethics is more realistic. It calls

CREATION AND PROCESS

on each person to recognize that growth and personal development demand wrestling with contradiction and tension. According to an ecumenical morality the struggle with self asociated with conflicting images of abortion is a positive religious reality. Tension, trauma, and conflict can be religiously affirmed as a basis of human achievement rather than denied.

The religious meaning of conflict should be celebrated as are all stages of human development. A special blessing to mark an abortion might seem odd at first glance. Yet each woman must realize how problematic is her assertion each day, "Praised art Thou O Lord for creating me according to your Will," (man is known to thank God who "has not created me a woman!"). She will realize the need to acknowledge struggle and to sanctify *becoming* and change. An ecumenical *Halakhah* must find new religious forms to express this new insight and bend traditional ones to represent it more fully. A woman who has wrestled with the issue of abortion is certainly more creatively religious than one who has followed either tradition or modernity blindly. Her religious life is more responsive than that of a man whose understanding of the spiritual dimensions of childbirth is limited to legal injunctions.

An ecumenical morality of abortion is productive because it honestly reflects the trauma of woman's experience. While it may begin with definitions of pregnancy, birth, and woman's role given by a male tradition, it moves beyond that tradition. While attentive to the needs of modern women and their desires, it also recognizes how problematic modernity is to many women. This honest recogniton of the conflicted struggles of a modern Jewish woman is a positive contribution an ecumenical ethics can give to a woman seeking guidance about an unwanted pregnancy. A second advantage to an ecumenical approach is its flexibility. No realm of human experience lies outside the possibility of sanctification. Through dialogue with human life an ecumenical Judaism creates forms by which even the trauma of abortion can be a religious affirmation .Ritual and prayer can serve the individual and elevate daily struggle into cosmic insight. Because an ecumenical ethics is not limited to traditional rituals it can sanctify abortion by giving it a place in a modern ritual system.

An Ecumenical Halakhah: Humility, Trust, and Sanctification

What, then, is the persuasive argument for an ecumenical interpretation of *Halakhah*? Can this new approach to Jewish ethics be justified as a valid modern alternative? An ecumenical *Halakhah* enables a Jew to make moral decisions in a world of changing natural forces. Although the Jew, like others in the modern world, cannot predict where human discoveries will lead or how human beings will transform nature, an ecumenical Judaism offers continuing guidance. While a traditional Judaism may find itself hard pressed to find relevant precedents for new situations, an ecumenical Judaism listens to modern needs and gives them a crucial part in ethical dialogue. While a subjective liberalism obscures the sharp outlines of Jewish morality, an ecumenical Judaism refuses to abandon basic principles or to escape confronting the concrete details of Jewish law. While a conservative modernism relies on an abstract ethical ideal, an ecumenical Jewish morality recognizes the real conflict which modern experience creates. *Halakhah* seen from the ecumenical perspective is an honest confrontation with both Judaism and modernity without expecting to discover a resolution to the conflicts involved.

CREATION AND PROCESS

The basic moral stance is traditional — morality consists of humility before God, trust in God's creation, and belief in humanity's ability to hallow life. The ecumenical perspective, however, claims that none of these principles are simple, that they are each complex and entail tension and conflict. Submission to God is hardly identical with obedience to received traditions. An ecumenical ethics admits the problems with accepting the admittedly suspect testimony of human beings as the unalterable word of God. Modernity is as fallible as human understanding of divine will is tradition. The ecumenical approach says that true humility submits to the divine will whether that will is heard in tradition or in the experiences of daily life. Trust in God's creation is an ambiguous value since part of that creation entails the human ability to alter and transform nature. The ecumenical perspective claims that *Halakhah* is a process. Trust must be placed in the direction of growth, the movement of development rather than in any particular "natural order." Ecumenical ethics seeks an ongoing learning about God's creation rather than an implicit trust in a humanly determined set of "natural laws." This trust in process means that societies no less than individuals must experiment. A social program now justified may become obsolete in the near future. An ecumenical approach urges caution in institutionalizing a passing social need as an enduring human truth. The path of process must be kept open even if civil necessity may require temporary legislation.

Human beings sanctify life by making choices, by acknowledging their conflicts and tensions. An ecumenical ethics refuses to hide the confusion which plagues modern people. Life is sanctified only if it is affirmed in all its ambiguity. Real life must be made holy, not an idealized hope which is made to pass for that life. An ecumenical *Halakhah* answers the modern dilemma about nature. Nature is not demonic, neither is humanity. Nature is not holy in itself, neither are human beings. Through interaction nature and humanity sanctify each other — holiness arises out of the trauma of conflict and meeting.

CHAPTER THREE
SOCIAL RESPONSIBILITY AND COVENANT

Modernity and Social "Mitzvah"

An ecumenical Jewish ethics insists that moral decisions be made in the social as well as the natural sphere. Human beings control political forces no less destructive than scientific power. The Jewish concept of *Mitzvah* entails obligations to the community, obligations that have social and political implications. Jews are concerned with the extended social effects of their actions. The goal of Judaism is a community of service to God. Such a society is more than parochial since all humanity is included in it. The Jew strives to do more than improve Jewish life; the task is *tikkun olam*, improvement of the world. Jews justify their survival on more than chauvinistic claims; God legitimates Jewish life only when it is lived for the sake of humanity. Jewish social obligation is involved with all human society. Jews fulfill their destiny when they live distinctively among the nations of the world and improve the total life of all humanity.

This traditional justification of Jewish distinctiveness as *tikkun olam* is suspect in the modern world. Modern experience has shown how self-serving such idealistic principles can be. The tradition assumes that good is possible because it is commanded: "God placed the good in the world as a moral demand which man is able to fulfill."[1] The modern Jew is skeptical of such an assumption. Putative good, supposed "moral demands" may mask self-interest, may disguise demonic and inhumane programs of aggression.

Modern Jews doubt the traditional understanding of *Mitzvah* and *tikkun olam* because of a realistic appraisal of social life. Political institutitons have been shown demonically corrupt. Even moral individuals fall prey to communal evil. Traditionally, Jews have mitigated the self-serving elements possible in claims to Jewish chosenness by reference to *Mitzvah and tikkun olam*. Jews are chosen for a task; they are obligated to pursue a universalistic and humanistic goal. The particularism of Jewish identity, the exclusivism of *Torah* as a peculiarly Jewish teaching, the distinctiveness of Jewish society have all been justified as a means to reach beyond Jewish parochialism to a truly international human fellowship. These claims can now be suspected in the light of the lofty principles in the name of which societies created Auschwitz, Hiroshima, and Viet Nam.

If Jews are to affirm their chosen task it must be in a more concretely universal way than traditionally understood. Task must be more evidently humanistic than Jews have seen it before. The vague hopes and messianic expectations of traditional Jews must become undisputably humanistic *in effect* as well as in theory. Although the idea of chosenness is *social* the litmus test of the idea must be the individual. John Roth, reflecting on the lessons of the Nazi Holocaust, understands this paradox. He claims that the concept of being chosen must be justified by its effect on an individual's life. "After Auschwitz," he insists, "the only way in which it can make good sense to say that a group or an individual is chosen is if that conviction leads men to empty themselves in service that meets human need."[2] Social obligation is judged by how it influences an individual.

The first lesson of a modern view of covenant is that the individual must suspect all social institutions. No matter how idealistic or exalted, any institution can be perverted and made to serve selfish ends. Any concept of social obligation that depends on absolute trust, submission, or unquestioned obedience to political institutions is immediately unreliable. The lessons of modernity mean that "membership in a political community is no longer a guarantee of the most elemental human rights."[3] Unlike the traditional approach to *Mitzvah* a modern view must distrust all political forms. Communal ideals need to be understood as contingent, not absolute, values. Obligations must be set in particular contexts, and regarded as relative expectations which can be flexible and responsive to changing human needs. An absolutized value can easily become destructive.

The second lesson is that parochial self-assertion can easily parade as universalism. In Jewish life Zionism has often demonstrated this possibility. Of course many very real social and political necessities have made Zionism an indispensable modern option for many Jews. When, however, that option is presented as an idealistic, utopian ideal for all humanity, when it is disguised as *tikkun olam*, results can be disastrous. The Zionist who masks political pragmatism in spiritual language, who justifies imperialism and aggression by reference to exalted ideals, has cheapened Jewish religious life. Hannah Arendt charts how Zionist ideals were made to serve a destructive nationalism. Rather than motivate service of others, Zionist propaganda obscured the self-serving and chauvanistic elements in Israeli life.[4]

Here we have two objections to traditional Judaism. The traditional understanding of covenant is untenable because it creates an absolutism which ignores the modern lesson of human deceit. Because tradition unquestionably accepts the social ideals inherited from the past, it trusts these political ideals as safeguards of human rights. Modernity has taught that only a flexible and self-doubting social vision can prevent abuse of power. Secondly, universalistic language can draw attention away from chauvinistic actions. Traditional Jewish idealism can justify acts of imperialism and terrorism. Because the ideal itself is unquestionably humanistic, the actual practice of Jewish nationalism is often falsely legitimated. The institutions of Jewish life — whether Zionist political power in the State of Israel or self-appointed representatives of Judaism in the diaspora — obscure their own powerbase and selfish aims under the mask of Jewish values. Until Jewish institutions are forced to be open to the challenge of their own self-interest they cannot motivate selfless humanism.

An ecumenical ethics might create a social morality which would meet these objections. Drawing on the traditional values of covenant and social obligation a dialectical morality can be created. Covenant is the source of both *Mitzvah* and *tikkun olam*. At its most simple covenant means mutual obligation; traditionally it refers to the reciprocal relationship between God and the holy community. The detailed obligations of this relationship are

Mitzvah; the visionary goal animating these obligations is *tikkun olam*. Because the relationship is dynamic the covenantal model is one of growth and development. *Mitzvah* grows out of the immediacy of encounters; *tikkun olam* provides fleeting and changing glimpses of that world which humanity can hope to reach.

In a modern context covenant refers to the shared responsibility of all members of the human community to develop productive and humane social structures. Covenant as a divine gift is the possibility, indeed, the indispensability and inevitability of interhuman exchange. *Mitzvah* arises from the obligations which flow from that exchange; *tikkun olam* is achieved when the pluralistic vision of an interconnected humanity becomes more and more realized in human social life. The two implications of this view provide answers to the objections raised against traditional Jewish thought. The first implication is that the Jew belongs to the human community no less than to a parochial Jewish group. The Jew contributes to world civilization through this double citizenship. Because the Jew has a special resource for social reflection the world community benefits. As a member of the human covenant the Jew has a religious obligation to participate in ecumenical dialogue. Secondly, the dynamic mutuality of covenant means that Jewish institutions must be attentive to the changing needs of human community. *Tikkun olam* is achieved by progressive development; rather than being a static ideal imposed on every situation, the vision it projects is gradually realized through reciprocal living. Social institutions must be flexible and responsive if the ideal hidden in each situation is to be realized. Jewish instituitons learn through covenant to distrust themselves, to suspect an absolutism which can corrode the structure of covenantal life itself. When reciprocal obligation is replaced by authoritarian dogma and blind obedience, covenant has been subverted. For a modern Jew *tikkun olam* is impossible when pluralistic possibilities are denied through an insular and unbending traditionalism.

In this covenental theology of social responsibility the objections to traditional views of Jewish chosenness are answered. The danger of isolationism is avoided by making *Mitzvah* a relational and reciprocal duty. *Mitzvah* evolves from situations, from dialogue. Since covenant is with all of humanity, no one perspective, no single traditional set of *mitzvoth* can comprehend those duties which are immediately relevant. The Jew must remain distinctive and must cultivate an independent identity in order to *respond* to changing demands rather than to preserve an unchanging reality. *Mitzvah* does include a proud affirmation of self; a Jewish duty is indeed that of remaining recognizably different from the non-Jew. Such difference, however, is for the sake of interaction. Jewish communal distinctiveness is not an end in itself but a means for reaching out to others in a changing world. The Jew fulfills *Mitzvah* by entering the arena of world politics and affirming membership in the extended society of humanity. Such political activism, however, would be meaningless without a specific Jewish contribution to social dialogue. The Jew remains distinctive in order to have a unique perspective to share with others. That perspective alone, however, is only part of *Mitzvah*. *Mitzvah* is fulfilled in the dynamic context of social dialogue.

Each Jew has the *Mitzvah* of entering into social dialogue. The Jewish people as a whole — expresssed through concrete Jewish institutions — has social responsibilities of its own. These obligations demand self-critical examination. A Jewish society cannot remain content with its inherited values, established power, or legitimated leadership. Self-doubt is the creative stimulus for change and development. If *tikkun olam* is dynamic and progressive, then Jewish chauvinism contradicts the ideals of Jewish religious obligation. Covenental thinking means that the Jewish political order must change as the world develops. No unchanging political structure can go uncriticized. No political decision, no legal enactment, no demand for loyalty or support is unconditionally right, inalterably true, unassailably absolute. Jewish institutions — whether national, lobby groups, local leadership contingents, or regional communities — must as part of covenantal awareness acknowledge their limitations. An ecumenical ethics demands that social obligations be refined through the process of dialogue. Monolithic social or political structure contradicts this ethics. Ecumenical thinking is a safeguard against chauvinism and the perversion of ideals by cultivating self-analysis and doubt.

Modern Views of Covenant

This ecumenical approach to covenant must be tested against authentic Jewish tradition. How have modern Jews understood covenant? Is the ecumenical view compatible with both modernity and Judaism? Such an examination of the concept is difficult because there is no unambiguous view of covenant in Jewish tradition. Even the biblical record shows how the royal tradition of King David manipulated covenantal religion and how the prophetic tradition responded by its own very different view of covenant. Among the prophets themselves covenant was understood in diverse ways. Perhaps the complexity and variety in covenantal religion is itself important. Certainly later Judaism which stressed the differences and the compatibility between the Noahide, Abrahamic, and Mosaic covenants found value in variety. Modern approaches continue this appreciation of differences but sees them in the light of the dramatic events shaping contemporary Judaism.

Modern Jewish thinkers defend covenant by showing the failure of modern social life. Jewish social values may seem parochial or self-serving; when tested against the reality of human politics they demonstrate their persuasiveness. The defence offered by Jews from differing standpoints — traditionalist, liberal, conservative modern — is essentially unified: Judaism as represented by covenant, *Mitzvah* and *tikkun olam* is a relevant answer to modern problems. Modernity is only an apparent contradiction to Jewish social thought. The problems with traditional values are merely superficial; upon examination Judaism appears a needed corrective to contemporary life.

Reformed Jewish theologian Eugene Borowitz recognizes that the experience of modern universalism makes Jewish distinctiveness difficult to acccept. He also agrees that modern history seems to imply "God's absence in the real affairs of men."[5] Nevertheless he claims modernity alone is bankrupt. Jews, he finds, are recognizing the inadequacy of contemporary answers to human problems and are returning to Jewish values. Losing faith in modern culture Jews reaffirm their moral tradition.[6]

This act of returning to a tradition of social values provides Borowitz with a key to the Jewish task — the meaning of Jewish chosenness. The Jew bears witness to the world that faith is still possible, that hope in the future is a realistic expectation. The atrocities of the past and the bleakness of the present seem to cast the modern

SOCIAL RESPONSIBILITY AND COVENANT

person into doom-expecting gloom. Borowitz feels that Jews can break this dismal spell by defending hope and the promise of the future. Secular arguments for hope have failed, but trust in God's promise is still a human possibility. Judaism's universal value lies in its ability to motivate trust in the future.[7]

Such trust is based on concrete experience. The Jew has faith in the future because the torture of Auschwitz became the glowing hope of the modern State of Israel. This new "theopolitical" form of Jewish life created a new set of possibilities for Jews. In that state Jews could develop new talents, explore new social options, and discover untried means of implementing God's plans. Borowitz sees the Israeli victory in June 1967 as undeniable confirmation of covenant — God still preserves Israel as a political experiment, as a resource for social and religious innovation in the modern world.[8] Although cynics explained that victory in purely secular terms, Borowitz sees it as a religious witness. God works for the oppressed, liberates the enslaved, and enables Jews to create a new political order. Because it occurred in the real world of national experience Israel's victory transformed the way in which Jews understood world history and their religious task.

Borowitz, then, emphasizes a psychology of hope. The Jew remains distinctive because in a modern, disillusioned world Judaism affirms hope; Jewish nationalism is more than parochial pride because through Israel's history the entire human community discovers the importance of "theopolitical" structures; Jewish faith is inextricable from Jewish politics for the latter is the foundation of the former, its concrete manifestation. Eliezer Berkovits, a tradititionalist, suggests the same defence of Jewish covenantal thought, but adds a more specific and detailed study of Jewish obligations. He looks at Jewish life during the Nazi Holocaust and the creation of the State of Israel from the perspective of Judaic precepts.

The problem posed by the Holocaust is the relevance of Jewish law in a time of violence and destruction. Surely modern Jews must question the viability of a way of life which led them like lambs to the slaughter. Berkovits agrees that the Holocaust provides examples of the depths to which human life can sink. He notes that the perversity of human nature was singularly evident in Nazi Germany. He claims, however, that Jews who kept *Torah* and *Halakhah* and practiced *Mitzvah* as a means of social survival witnessed to a high level of human spirituality. The Jew is heir to the greatness of Auschwitz, a greatness due in no small measure to Jewish obedience to traditional laws. "Nowhere else in this world," Berkovits notes, "and never before could one experience the nobility of existence as then and there."[9] Obedience to God's commandments in the face of tragedy and disaster transforms a human being. From being the helpless victim of circumstances, a person becomes an exemplar of a divine way. By continued devotion to a revealed social ideal the Jew even in the midst of human depravity demonstrates the glory of being a person. Covenant preserves an individual's humanity.

Jewish chosenness finds its universal relevance in this witness of human potential. Modern Judaism by affirming God in the face of the Holocaust is fulfilling its task of demonstrating that covenant is a beginning and history merely a collection of incidents. Auschwitz is not the end of Sinai but part of an ongoing series of events.[10] The Jew is chosen to witness that covenant gives history meaning; history does not refute covenant.

SOCIAL RESPONSIBILITY AND COVENANT

History cannot refute covenant because covenant is a reminder of God's priorities — not human ones. Human beings judge history by success, power, and victory. God, however, establishes covenantal standards — standards that value the weak and vulnerable. Covenant stands as a contradiction of human expectations. Human beings would expect God to choose the mighty and the powerful; covenant demonstrates that "God needs a small and relatively weak people."[11] Why is the divine need for the vulnerable? God chooses a nation not for its own sake but for the sake of others. Being God's people means being a barometer for humanity. Covenant implies that God has a relationship with this people because this people serves all humanity and stands in responsive mutuality with other nations. Berkovits looks at Jewish history, at the vulnerability of Jews throughout history, and finds in Jewish existence a "point for the crystallization of moral direction in history." The Jew is humanity's diagnostician. By looking at the Jew the world learns to know itself.[12]

Jews are chosen because they are responsive and not impervious to the realities of the world. The Jew serves humanity for God by accepting the impression of the world upon its own soul. If this is the case, then how can Jewish power be defended? Does the existence of a Jewish state contradict the meaning of covenant? Berkovits declares that the State of Israel is a modern necessity. Its existence testifies to God's desire for a national Jewish home. The modern world consists of political states. The Jew can respond to that world only as a political body and not merely as a religious group. God, Berkovits insists, cannot "in this post-holocaust phase of world history, do without Israel, the state."[13] If the Jew is to serve as God's barometer of humanity it can do so in the modern world only as a nation state.

While Berkovits represents a traditional view and Borowitz a liberal interpretation of covenant, Elliot Dorff follows the conservative modernist approach, noting the restlessness of modern thinkers with the idea of covenant. Some Jewish writers defend the concept pragmatically. The benefits of Jewish self-identification outweigh the drawbacks of parochialism. Other Jews use a subjective, existential legitimation of the concept. Covenental demands for social deeds, ritual performance, and even communal loyalty are seen as expressions of a developing self. The energy used to defend covenant — whether naturalistically or existentially — testifies to its importance. Dorff calls covenant the central concept around which all of Jewish life must be organized.[14]

Two complementary aspects of Judaism emerge from covenant. The first is the structure of personal identity. The Jewish way of life provides an authoritative guide to how and in what way one is a Jew. Each Jew is uniquely recognizable because of adherence to traditional ways of behavior. Ethnic identity is rooted less in custom and heredity than in common allegiance to a revealed legislation. Jewish hopes and aspirations — the messianic expectation for an improved world — are animated and given concrete meaning by Jewish law.[15]

Judaism also emphasizes the universal aspects of covenant. Tradition bridges the gap between parochial and universalistic thinking. Nowhere is this ability to comprehend opposites more apparent than in covenant as an *historical* category. Covenant has been the historical catalyst transforming Jews from individuals into members of a collectivity. By accepting covenant a Jew associates with the joy and pain, sacrifice and exaltation of

Jewish life. Covenant implies that selfishness is set aside for the sake of the general good. The idea of covenant may include a stress upon identity and parochial self-recognition. It is also the basis for reaching out towards others, moving beyond the self to a sense of fellowship and mutuality with others.[16]

This all-inclusiveness means that a narrow definition of "religious values" cannot be adequate for an understanding of Jewish covenant. Covenant may have a religious aim, it may express spiritual joy. It also embraces ethnic elements which grow out of "secular" experience. The hallowing of the everyday is an important part of covenantal life. Dorff advocates recognizing the sanctity of the "nonreligious" elements in Jewish life. Covenant cannot be forced into an alien mold. Its stance of faith expands beyond preconceived religiosity.

An Ecumenical Perspective on Covenant

There is surprising agreement in these three views of covenant. First, each author argues that pride in Jewish identity is an essential part of covenant. Borowitz sees that pride as a reaction against modern pessimism; Berkovits identifies it with traditional Jewish observance; Dorff points to the way Jewish life is patterned in a recognizable way. Second, all three writers find the universal meaning of Judaism to lie in its applicability to all humanity. Borowitz sees Jews conveying the gift of hope to a disillusioned world; Berkovits exalts Jews as God's human barometer; Dorff sees in the communal nature of covenant a lesson in transcending selfishness. Finally, the modern State of Israel, the secular and ethnic elements of Jewish life, are bound up intimately with Jewish faith. Borowitz sees in the State of Israel a concrete sign of human possibilities; Berkovits hails that state as a signal of God's need for human politics; Dorff includes "nonreligious" aspects of Judaism as part of covenant. A traditional understanding of covenant, then, will emphasize Jewish parochial identity, universal elements arising from that parochialism, and communal solidarity as part of personal faith. This traditional emphasis, however, is problematic in the modern world. Pride in identity often leads to nationalistic aggression; universal values are corrupted by human evil into masks for self-interest; the lure of solipsistic self-indulgence defeats the lofty goals of personal religion. Traditionalist, liberal, and conservative modernists seek to defend Jewish values. In the face of modern experience they affirm Judaic covenant.

An ecumenical approach would accept the problematic nature of Judaism. Covenant would be less a solution to the problems of Jewish life than a means of constantly being reminded of them. Modern experience should be allowed to challenge Jewish life, but Jewish life should also be able to challenge modernity. The demonic side of nationalism, human nature, or the personal dimension of social life is not the full story of human potential. A dialogue between the promises made by Jewish expectations and the realistic pessimism of an age of Auschwitz can stimulate creative social ethics. Jewish group-consciousness can be an uneasy recognition of both the inescapability of parochial identity and the necessity of expanding that consciousness to include identification with those different from ourselves. Jewish universalism can affirm human potential despite the harsh lessons of modernity by suggesting that humanity's survival depends on an interlocking network of institutions. Personal religion is an ambivalent gift. On the one hand it roots identity in loyalty to a communal order. On the other hand it can be justified only as a vital, intensely individual, response to the immediacy of divine address.

These ways of approaching nationalism, human nature, and personal religion are reflected in Jewish tradition. That tradition uses covenantal imagery to express such a perspective on social obligation. The three covenantal figures Abraham, Noah, and Moses mirror an ecumenical vision of communal duties. Jewish community as such can well be characterized as Mosaic. Rabbinic teaching notes the ambiguity of tracing Judaism to Moses. Moses is both the humblest of men and the unquestioned legal authority. Mosaic community affirms religious ideals as absolute values while maintaining a chastening humility born of self-doubt. Noah — from whom all post-deluvian humanity descends — was an equally ambivalent ancestor. Although worthy of being saved from a flood, his actions upon being saved caused God to lament that man's impulse is evil from birth. Noahide covenant is born from this recognition of humanity's duality. God establishes covenant with Noah to protect the world from human beings no less than to protect human beings in themselves. The Noahide image is ironic — covenantal expectations of humanity arise from a realistic appraisal of human weakness and corruptibility! Finally Judaism as a religious tradition looks backward to Abraham as the "father of faith." Abraham is regarded as the first Jew — but a Jew who *anticipated* Mosaic law, living its communal order as a private individual. Abraham is symbolic of the group, but representative of the individual. The covenant with Abraham is made for the sake of that nation which Abraham's descendents shall become. It is made, however, with Abraham alone. The solitary believer, the person of faith, is the foundation upon which social identity depends. Without the individual the society is impossible; without society the individual cannot inherit faith.

Mosaic Covenant: An Ecumenism of Jewish Life

Moses is the rabbinic model, par excellence, as his title, "Moses, our rabbi," clearly indicates. Mosaic covenant establishes community through laws and structure. A wandering collection of ex-slaves becomes united through Mosaic legislation. Only by obedience to Moses do the escaped remnants from Egyptian slavery discover how to be free. The irony is that by following a new law, the Hebrews become liberated. Martin Buber understood this paradox. God needs authoritative leaders who institute specific regulations for a community. Without the firm structure of these regulations citizens would be abandoned to their impulses. From being slaves to an external tyrant they would be slaves to an internal one —unchecked desire. If authority is taken away from these communal leaders, Buber suggests, then "the actual dominion is take away from God."[17] The authenticity of Jewish life depends upon an attitude of obedience. Jews live authentically when they vitalize their connection with those leaders who mold Jewish identity according to divine decree.

Jewish identitiy is not free; not every one who claims to be a Jew can be acknowledged as one. Being a Jew means being willing to accept an external measure of one's life. Taking a name means taking a responsibility as well. Samson Raphael Hirsch caught this emphasis by declaring that "whatever the period of the circumstance in which you live, it is the Torah that must determine your course of life for you."[18] An individual earns the right to be called a Jew. A name which can mean all things to all

SOCIAL RESPONSIBILITY AND COVENANT 65

people has little usefulness. Authoritative leadership determines the broad framework within which the term "Jew" can be meaningfully used.

The necessity to limit the way in which "Jew" can be used does not necessarily entail accepting a traditionalist stand. Criteria for authoritative and authentic leadership differ among various modern Jewish groups. The principle being advocated here is that one aspect of Jewish self-identification must be acceptance of some external gauge of authenticity. A Jew who denies Judaism the right to veto the shape of choices made, if not particular choices, has effectively denied the power of Jewish religion. A Jewish life without recognizably Jewish social obligations is hardly a helpful self-definition. The question of which elements in Judaism are determinative can be argued. Eugene Borowitz has a right to claim that despite his affirmation of personal freedom, he has accepted Jewish authority. He allows Judaism a decisive say in his self-understanding and so asserts that "I still manage to believe enough . . . I can still go to meet my God as one of his covenanted people."[19] Covenant means taking the definition of community and social obligation seriously enough to change actions because of it. Acceptance of authoritative leadership is a prerequisite for any Jewish claim to be part of the covenant community.

An ecumenical approach to Mosaic covenant must begin with this acceptance of authority and then move beyond it toward open dialogue. Can this movement be made? Can authority and ecumenism be reconciled? Perhaps Jewish self-definition itself includes a dialogical component. If being a Jew entails reaching out to non-Jews, then accepting the authority of Jewish tradition means a readiness to call that authority into question when it endangers the ability to enter into dialogue with others.

This ecumenical approach seems anticipated in a statement by Rabbi Akiva, an early mishnaic teacher. Akiva expresses the idea of Jewish chosenness in connection with humanity's exalted station in general. He claimed that humanity is blessed by being created in God's image and especially blessed by being made aware of having been so created. Jews are singled out because they are blessed with being called God's children and with being made aware of that blessing (Avot 3:14). What is the special blessing that awareness brings? Being aware of one's station means a greater readiness to fulfill the obligations of that station. Human beings can actualize the divine image because they are aware of it; Jews can realize the potential of their relationship to God because it has been made known to them.

What particular duties are associated with being a child of God? Certainly one obligation a child owes to its parents is that of acknowledging them. One aspect of Mosaic covenant involves an acknowledgement of divine parentage. The Jew is to be holy as God is holy; Jewish life is lived "al kiddush ha-shem," for the sanctification of God. The Jew lives a recognizable life because through that life God is recognized. Jews obey certain restrictive laws, become part of a separate community, and follow a distinctive political order, in self-confessed loyalty to their divine parent. Jewish identity follows a predictable, patterned continuity because the divine source of that identity is eternal, unchanging, continuous.

A second duty falling to a child is that of imitaton of the parent. The parent provides a model which the child puts into practice. The child extends the ideals, values and hopes of the parent into new spheres of activity. The Jew imitates the divine parent in the same way. One of the responsibilites of Jewish identity is following in the footsteps of the divine. This type of imitation of God means reaching out to others — feeding the hungry, clothing the naked, burying the dead. As God reaches out to all human beings, so the Jew in imitation of the divine is to enter a dialogue with others. An ecumenical ethics will affirm covenantal obligation when parochial identity includes as one of its requirements self-exposure to those outside the covenantal community. Mosaic covenant is predicated on Israel's relation to God as parent. That relationship means that no authority or legislation can obstruct the Jew's dialogic interaction with other human beings.

Mosaic covenant is a model of parochial identity which by its very nature expands beyond parochialism. Nationalism is often destructive because it is imperialistic. God's nature, however, prevents such imperialism. God's actions are directed toward others; creation itself is a negation of imperialism in favor of pluralism. Mosaic covenant insists that a society is false to its divine origin if it seeks to abandon pluralism and impose a monolithic structure on the human community. The essence of Mosaic covenant is God's desire for a variety of diverse covenantal communities. Religion, Martin Buber suggests, cannot be understood in the abstract. Only particular religions have meaning. Each individual religious community represents "the relationship of a particular human community as such" to God.[20] An ecumenical ethics would answer the challenge of chauvinism with this built-in dialogic element of Mosaic covenant.

Mosaic covenant points to the social responsibility of

each Jew to maintain the particularity of Jewish identification. Were a Jew to avoid the embarrassing peculiarities of Judaism, that would be an evasion of covenantal obligation. Were a Jew to deny the particularity of the Jewish experience that would betray the meaning of Jewish identity. At the same time a withdrawal into isolationism would equally be a betrayal and evasion. Since Jewish communal identity is founded on an imitation of God, any self-restriction is unsupportable. God's universalism provides a model of Jewish action. Only be reaching out beyond Jewish community can a Jew actualize the duties of Jewish communal life. Abraham Joshua Heschel understood this ecumenical sense of parochial duty well. The Jewish task, he suggests, it "to unite what lies apart, to remember that humanity as a whole is God's beloved child."[21] The title that Rabbi Akiva limited to Jews, Heschel extends to all humanity. Certainly he does so justifiably. When a traditional authority would challenge such an approach (and Akiva, as we shall see, was once so challenged) it must give way. The principle of imitating God transcends any particular detail of traditional authority.

What, then, is an ecumenical view of nationalism? Based on the ideal of Mosaic covenant it asserts that the Jew has two social obligations based on the distinctive nature of Jewish culture. The first obligation is that of maintaining Judaism as a recognizable element in social life. The Jew is not to obliterate or obscure the distinctly Jewish aspects of communal organization found in traditional Judaism. The marks of Jewish life — loyalty to the Jewish community, refusal to abandon distinctive Jewish ways, responsibility to support Jewish life where and when it is threatened — are affirmed. The second obligation entails imitating God's ecumenical reaching out to all

SOCIAL RESPONSIBILITY AND COVENANT

of humanity. The Jewish task is that of entering into dialogue with non-Jews, sharing Jewish insights with others, and fulfilling obligations to other human beings where they are in need.

An ecumenical understanding of Mosaic covenant sees it as a creative mixture of parochial identity and universal impulses. Just because the Jew is distinguishable and different, society is enriched. Mosaic covenant contributes its tension between the recognition that all human beings are God's children and its Jewish self-affirmation as a productive model of social identity. Parochial and particularistic aspects of a culture must not be sacrificed for the purpose of peace and quiet. A society sacrifices its richness and resources by doing so. Social responsibility, however, demands that minority cultures extend themselves beyond their own confines. The purpose of cultural independence is the cultural exchange throughout the entire society that results. Mosaic covenant is an ecumenical model of self-assertion for the sake of dialogue and contribution to others.

Noahide Covenant: The Human Possibility of Ecumenical Meeting

Mosaic covenant assumes that ecumenical meeting is possible. Pluralism is creative only if differing cultural groups can share with one another. Modern experience suggests that an optimistic expectation of such sharing is unwarranted. Human selfishness undermines the attraction of the ideal which community presents. In the midst of the modern crisis and its revelations about human nature is dialogue a genuine possibility? Traditionally Jews give an affirmative answer based on their theological trust. Because all human beings stand under the legislation given by God to Noah they are members of one unified community. Even the covenant at Sinai, Mosaic covenant, does not supercede but merely augments Noahide community. Jews share with non-Jews the common human responsibilities symbolized by the Noahide covenant. This commonality is the basis for a united task, a genuine dialogue. Robert Gordis argues that this Noahide universalism is a unique Jewish contribution to national and international politics. On the basis of Noahide law a universal social ethics can be built.[22]

The realities of political life after Auschwitz, Hiroshima, and Viet Nam make a traditional affirmation of Noahide community impossible. That affirmation assumed a concensus on values and social concerns which modern history shows nonexistent. A nontraditional approach, however, can use Noah as an example of general humanity without suggesting that the details of Noahide legislation become the basis for all social life. While Mosaic covenant does depend upon adherence to the details of traditional life, Noahide covenant is powerful as a symbol, even if its specifics are disregarded. The attitude of common human obligation is more important than a specific designation of that obligation. The figure of Noah rather than the laws of Noah are essential. That figure is a suggestive one. Noah was the quintessential survivor; the basic human obligation is that of surviving.

Noah is a survivor three times over. First, he is a survivor of the corrupting influence of decaying civilization. Noah lives in a time of human depravity and moral corruption. He manages to survive the polluting influence of his age and retains his purity. He refuses to accept the moral precepts of his time and transcends his environmental conditioning. He survives the social determinism which seems to grip every individual overwhelmed by the social

SOCIAL RESPONSIBILITY AND COVENANT 71

process. Second, Noah is a survivor in the midst of other survivors. He survives his isolation from others through his task of ministering to the animals who survive God's punishment. Not only does he survive uncorrupted by his environment, but his escape from disaster is also a test of his ability. He withstands the challenges offered by surviving and being responsible for the survival of others. He survives his duties no less than the threats of his social setting. Survival is tested by the tasks one must perform as well as the contest in which one must perform them. Finally, Noah survives his own foolishness. According to the biblical story and its rabbinic explanations Noah's first act after surviving the flood was an act of folly. He planted a vineyard, cultivated it, drank wine, and was sexually abused. Despite this folly he continued as a patriarch, spoke words of prophecy and power, and retained his religious status. Survival means to survive one's own stupidity. Human beings have besetting vices — they succumb to temptation, they are victims of abuse. The Noahide image suggests that they can survive even their own errors, their own self-wrought wounds.

Covenant has a universal implication when understood as a category of survival. The Jew transforms a particularistic image — that of Noah — into an illustration of human nature and thereby contributes a cause for hope and trust in the future. Humanity, seen through the Noahide prism, is not perfect, has many flaws, but will survive. Humanity survives because through covenanted relationship it can retain its ideals in the midst of social chaos, survive its obligations in a time of trial, and survive its own mistakes despite human foolishness.

The Jew learned this lesson of survivorship through the Nazi Holocaust. During this period of dark despair, the

Jew discovered a reason for hope. One such reason has already been pointed out by Eliezer Berkovits — despite inhuman conditions the Jew could humanize them by obeying Jewish law. The ability of ideals to survive a destructive environment is thereby affirmed. Jews could come through the Holocaust experience with their faith intact; some who entered as unbelievers discovered faith through their trials and survival. Not only Jews but non-Jews as well discover hidden reservoirs of humanity, ideals and moral strength precisely when conditions seem least supportive.

A second reason is that survival under Nazi domination was made possible by ongoing human relations. Jews discovered that they could enter into real human relationships with one another even though the Nazis tried to strip them of their humanity. Human dignity found human task and social ties even in the death camps: "The depth and durability of man's social nature may be gauged by the fact that conditions in the concentration camps were designed to turn prisoners against each other; but that in a multitude of ways, men and women persisted in social acts."[23]

The third reason for hope lay in the double legacy of the Holocaust — a legacy of faith and rebellion. Some Jews found faith in the death camps, others found only emptiness. The modern Jew has inherited both the martyr's strength and the rebel's doubt.[24] Both go together and the modern Jew knows that human existence is an ambivalent, unclear actuality. Hope depends on recognizing failure and human weakness as well as expecting to find human strength. The Holocaust teaches the Jew that even human evil cannot destroy human good. Human doubt does not destroy the possibility of survival. Human

SOCIAL RESPONSIBILITY AND COVENANT 73

beings can transcend their own limitations, and survive their own self-doubt.

The Jew emerges from Auschwitz with a new Noahide message — human beings are survivors. The universal message of the Jew is that covenant binds all human beings together by a common humanity rather than by a universal law. The unity of human society lies in attitudes rather than specific, detailed instructions. Human beings survive because society itself has certain inevitable characteristics — ideals persist even when conditions seem to negate them; human beings reach out to one another even when deprived of every suppport and stay; human evil and weakness cannot destroy an individual, self-transcendence is always a real possibility.

Does the idea of covenant contribute to human social life? If the contribution must be measured in specific details and legislations the answer must be no. The universalism of an ecumenical view of covenant lies in its message about human nature. Human ability to survive becomes the basic contention which a Jew contributes to ongoing social discussions. Noahide covenant implies that social institutions must coexist in a positive environment of growth and mutuality. Trusting in the interactional basis of human life each institution must grant to each other the right of experimentation and social development. The Noahide lesson is that of respect — any imperialistic institutional attempt at self-aggrandizement is suspect since it denies the human worth of other institutions. An autocratic and authoritarian institutional life can only be justified on the basis of a pessimistic and thereby limited view of human potential. While individual religious groups have the right to their own particular social structures — indeed as seen above that right is a basic social need — they must also grant individual human choice and allow the existence and validity of alternative social institutions. Noahide covenant teaches that no social organization is bereft of values, no human failure is irrevocable, no social situation too desperate to benefit humanity, unless it becomes so absolute and authoritarian that it precludes the challenges offered by other social bodies. The lesson of Noahide teaching, then, is the necessity for inter-institutional trust based upon a realistic but optimistic appraisal of human nature. That universalistic view of social life and the possibilities of human achievement remains an important element in an ecumenical Judaism and is the foundation of a reconciliation between traditional affirmations and the stark realities of social and political existence discovered through contemporary events.

Abraham: Covenant with the Individual

Loyalty to social obligation requires personal sacrifice. The individual must place private needs behind public good. The idea of covenant is a persuasive symbol of the importance of such self-sacrifice. In Jewish tradition the patriarch Abraham symbolizes that person whose sense of self depends upon a social consciousness. Abraham has been promised future greatness — but that greatness will be social, not personal. Abraham's life is guided by a vision of a national destiny, a destiny which he begins but cannot see the end of. Abraham, in his religious loyalty and dedication to the people that his descendants will become, is representative of Jewish religion. Much is required of the indivdual; personal faith is often put to the test. The richness of religious life depends on inner experience, and private devotion. For the Jew that inner religiousness is possible only through a vital relationship

SOCIAL RESPONSIBILITY AND COVENANT

with other Jews, and Jewish nationality.

The duality involved in this religiousness creates a personal ambivalence found also in the stories about Abraham. Dorothy Zeligs intuits Abraham's character using psycho-analytic models.[25] She rightly sees that Abraham is an ambivalent parent. On the one hand, his hopes and expectations are for the future. He invests the emotion of religious feeling in his children. Yet he willingly sacrifices those children for the sake of immediate religious experience. When God demands that one child be exiled, Abraham obeys. When God calls upon Abraham to sacrifice his child of promise, parental instincts are stifled. Religious identity in the present is rooted in a future social vision; the validity of future society, however, depends upon its loyalty to that vision.

Abraham is a model of Jewish ambivalence — the individual lives for the sake of ideal society, but society is judged by the individual using the measure of that ideal. The American Jew's relationship to the State of Israel mirrors a similar ambivalence. Jewish identity is nourished by the existence of that state. Each individual Jew finds personal roots in Israel and affirms Judaism by associating with modern Israeli society. Marshall Sklare points out that although Judaism could survive if Israel were destroyed, the psychological damage to American Jewish self-image "could be devastating."[26] The reason for such a catastrophic reaction, of course, is that Israel symbolizes American Jewry's ideals and values. Parades on Israeli independence day celebrate the possibility of a nonchauvinistic nationalism. Festivals of Israeli music, drama, dance, and culture manifest a social selfhood that contributes to world civilization. American Jews see their best hopes reflected in Israel's accomplishments.[27]

The American Jew is ambivalent toward the State of Israel because its real political activity often conflicts with the idealized picture. Israeli politics often dictates an inflexible position on religious and social issues. Military strategy often contradicts humanistic principles of humane treatment for enemies, self-sacrifice for the sake of peace, and conciliatory relations with hostile neighbors. Arthur Waskow recognizes this problem and despite his appreciation of how the Zionist approach has enabled Jews to recapture their own identity, he finally rejects it. The lessons of Jewish pride need to be tempered with religious insight. He suggests a dialogical process in which conflicting Zionist positions would wrestle with each other and with ideal religious values.[28] Loyalty to Israel would be persuasive only so long as it preserved a concrete relationship to those social ideals which animate Jewish religious hope.

American Jews should preserve their ambivalence towards the State of Israel. Abrahamic covenant implies just such ambiguity towards any concrete social or political group. The meaning of covenant in this context is the uneasy balance between personal loyalty to a group identity and faithfulness to the ideals imperfectly realized in that group. Covenant means relationship: on one level the relationship between traditional laws and parochial customs on the one hand and universal community on the other; on another level the relationship is between the realities of human nature and the equally real potential of any human collectivity; here the relationship is between the potential which informs group identity with meaning and the concrete reality of social organization which alone provides the vehicle by which potential is actualized. By its very nature such an approach to social and political obligation is ecumenical. Covenant means that no merely parochial or isolationist restriction or moral responsibility to one particular group is possible. Covenant means that all human beings must share in the responsibilities, possibilities, and potentials of social life. The failure of one person may mean the success of another. Dialogue alone can balance the relative strengths and weaknesses in every person. Finally covenant means that the individual must live in tension with social institutions. The individual must turn to others in dialogue and conversation as part of the process whereby political bodies are both accepted and challenged. The approach of modern Judaism to social and political morality is essentially ecumenical — only that social life which is open to dialogue on all levels is truly moral.

Social Mitzvah and Covenant: The Example of War

Can an ecumenical approach to social and political life illuminate some of the pressing problems of modernity? One such problem is that of violence — the violence of war and armed resistance. Many modern nations claim that their only chance for survival, for justice, for freedom and independence, lies in military revolution. Revolution, it can be plausibly argued, rectifies the injustice of tyrannical oppression, removes foreign aggression and imperialism, and redresses economic and civil wrongs. War can often be excused on the same basis. A nation seeks to preserve its liberty, independence, and ideology. Territorial boundaries become the basis for international self-defence. Loyalty to allies, the need to protect the weak, the obligation to fulfill treaties all seem reasonable arguments for military action.

Yet modernity has shown the extremes to which militarism can go. Countries have been devastated. Nuclear weapons have annihilated entire nations. Famine, deforestation, disease, and exile have ravaged whole populations. Even in the name of righteous causes the human suffering caused by war can hardly be justified. Perhaps it is better to follow those who advocate nonviolent resistance even at the cost of losing the battle than to win a war at such a price.

Jews face this issue when wrestling with their loyalty toward the state of Israel. Certainly the establishment of a Jewish homeland is necessary in the post-Holocaust world. Jews have no place of security, no social base for their communal life. In Israel this home was won by fighting, legal maneuvering, and even terrorism. The homeland has been maintained by means of ongoing battles, battles in which Israel's defensive moves often seemed strangely aggressive. The validity of self-preservation in this case often conflicted with inherited Jewish values. How, for example, are Jews to justify their wars when their own tradition states that God caused Israel to swear two solemn oaths — never to take the land of Israel by force, and never to rebel against the nations of the world.[29] This oath would seem to reject violent overthrow of any government and to exclude any military establishment of an Israeli Jewish state.

The question of Judaism and war must be raised and studied as part of covenantal ethics. The specific issues involved in a *Jewish* war concern the relationship of Jew to non-Jew, Jewish mission, and the religious witness given by modern Jews in general and the State of Israel in particular. Perhaps Israel's various wars are justified on social and ethical grounds. The war of Independence was fought on legal grounds; other wars were defensive, including a pre-emptive strike; still other wars fulfill the religious injunction to war against evil.[30]

SOCIAL RESPONSIBILITY AND COVENANT

Such a specific investigation, however, cannot ignore certain general principles. There is a strong pacifistic strain in Judaism which, while never dominant, must be considered. The humanity, even of the enemy, must be respected. Strong limitations were placed on a government's power to wage war. Every opportunity to resolve questions by peaceful means was used. Above all this the right of the indivdual to refuse to go to war for religious and social reasons — a right already present in the biblical injunctions of Deuteronomy — was recognized.[31]

War, from the Jewish perspective, must be regarded ambivalently. An ecumenical ethics would weigh the morality of war with a keen recognition of that ambivalence. Using the model of Mosaic covenant war must be understood both as an expression of national identity and also as a potentially demonic distortion of it. The morality of war does not consist in the religious ideology used to justify it. National self-assertion in itself is an ambiguous good; as a rationale for war it is a dubious virtue. The value of Jewish self-identification must be to continually raise doubts about the morality of any specific war. The example of Israeli soldiers in 1967 is instructive. Drawing on their own sense of Jewish religion they demanded "purity of arms." Only war which could meet the test of humane intention and ideal values could be accepted. At the end of the war there was as much lamenting over the dehumanizing aspects of war as over Israeli casualties.[32]

The American Jew faces a different problem. Judaism is represented by various factions, and differing social institutions. The question arising in America is the appropriateness of any institutional response to an American or Israeli war. Some objections are raised when a Jew embraces pacifism — either that Jew is self-hating and, therefore, willing to see Israel destroyed or that Jew brings a bad name of cowardice down upon all American Jews. The American Jew must defend the morality of pluralistic responses — even in the face of war. The Jewish task in the American setting is to insure that minority opinion is heard, that institutional dialogue occurs. The most devastating effect of war upon democracy is the enforced uniformity it produces. Divisions are set aside; a facade of unanimity is erected. The Noahide view of humanity refuses to abide by such a false impression. The Noahide covenant insists that difference is essentially productive; humanity has a chance when even failure is given its rightful place. No government has the right to usurp the individual's prerogative of choice. Only human interaction allows for that humane social living upon which survival depends.

Everett Gendler has pointed out that while Jewish precedent does support the right to make war it also claims that neither "moral decisions nor their bases are delegated to human authority in any unchallengeable way."[33] Judaism can survive only if Jewish institutions preserve the open environment for moral choice. Noahide survival asserts that human potential for good surpasses institutional authority. Only by learning the lesson that both human weakness and human ideals are present in every society can the disastrous potential of any war be mitigated.

War involves a decision about national identity and about the social structure which supports the war. Each individual, however, is confronted with a choice between war and pacifism. The modern Jew must follow the lead of Abraham who sometimes appears as a military hero and sometimes as a conciliatory diplomat. Some Jewish

SOCIAL RESPONSIBILITY AND COVENANT

authorities claim that Israel has a duty to destroy its Arab neighbors because their actions place them under the ban of Amalak.[34] Yet even the war against Amalek could be altered by personal conscience. Tradition is divided in evaluating Saul's decision to spare the Amalekite king. Perhaps mercy is more necessary than strict obedience to social convention.[35]

Abrahamic covenant suggests the Jew recognize personal ambivalence. War is neither an absolute evil nor an absolute social necessity. An individual who chooses for war may do so out of a variety of motives — social and personal needs blur when making the choice. Obligations to family, country, and the world intermingle with personal ambition, private fears, and moral doubts. Abrahamic covenant understands this complexity and recognizes that while social obligation may sometimes override personal desire, at other times personal religious vision must supplant social responsibility. An individual can be persuaded that war is right or wrong only on the basis of a dialogue between private and social values. Any attempt to impose an arbitrary absolutism — whether of the public good or of private independence — precludes genuine moral choice.

Social Morality and Ecumenical Ethics

From the standpoint of an ecumenical ethics social morality consists primarily in the command to distrust oneself as one distrusts society. The social world is filled with ambiguity. Personal and social identity intertwine — social morality demands a recognition of this mixture and an admission of the uncertain alloy that results. Moral decision cannot be legislated but must develop through dialogue among human beings. Social problems may demand an answer, but that answer cannot be made at the expense of ongoing discussion. A society that silences its minorities has lost a valuable resource and has violated its basic morality. Finally the interplay of personal and social values provides the individual with real moral choice. A society that denies the individual the right to moral decision has forfeited its claim to respect. A social morality that rejects personal freedom and denies the individual a chance to err has lost its persuasive power. In short, the yardstick by which an ecumenical ethics judges social morality is fidelity to the decision-making process as an ambiguous and conflicted human dilemma.

CHAPTER FOUR
SELFHOOD AND MITZVAH

Mitzvah, Personality, and Covenant

Mitzvah as social obligation entails recognizing the inevitable ambiguity of human decision-making. Whether reconciling modernity and tradition, structuring institutions, or determining the personal persuasiveness of social demands, *Mitzvah* requires acknowledging the uncertainty which plagues every human choice. An ecumenical view of personal morality will demand the same honest acceptance of the human situation. While an authoritarian traditionalism will solve the individual's dilemma by providing an unalterable model of personal development, an ecumenical morality will stress the self-doubt which makes all private decisions, even those made by an acceptance of an external ideal standard, suspect. While a libertarian affirmation of self-actualization legitimates all subjective decisions, an ecumenical morality will require that subjective motives be scrutinized and tested in relationship to received ideals and values. The essential aspect of an ecumenical morality will be the necessity of *choice* — neither personal desire nor traditional value can replace the precarious risk of moral choosing, or making decisions even in the midst of confusion.

Traditionalists, of course, would find this notion of choosing odd. Judaism is a religion of obedience, of revealed ideals which cannot be questioned on the basis of subjective human experience.[1] Indeed an ethics which allows subjective response can hardly be called a religious morality, according to some thinkers. Jacob Agus, for example, claims that "ethical values are obligatory for us because they are willed by a Supreme Will."[2] Moral worth depends on obedience to a revealed system derived from God's Will.

Since Immanuel Kant declared that only a self-legislated act could have moral worth Jews have been restless with their imposed moral revelation. A theonomous ethic, an ethic derived from an external divine Will, seems to undermine the moral value of Judaism. Some Jewish thinkers respond that Judaism does indeed value an autonomous act, an act freely chosen and freely performed. God's Will is actually the human will as it *ought to be*. Other Jewish thinkers decry this appeal to autonomy as rejecting Jewish presuppositions.[3] Perhaps the best way to understand the current situation is through recognizing its tension. Modern Jews look for guidance but still retain self-direction. Such a Jew "seeks a religious moral imperative but wants to remain open to the demands of each new situation."[4] The philosophical dialogue between the need for an absolute standard and the demand for personal responsibility and choice forms one foundation of a modern Jewish morality.

A second foundation is less philosophical than psychological. Choice is imperative not only as a result of the dialogue between religious ideals and human freedom but also because of the maturation process of each person. Personal development includes learning to reconcile inherited and internalized values with newly discovered potential and personal independence. Traditional Jewish symbol and myth, as Richard L. Rubenstein points out, understood this tension.[5] Yet modern Jewish approaches to personal morality seem to overlook it.

The traditional Jew uses *Halakhah* as a fixed model into which each individual personality must be made to fit. Sexual identity, personal decisions of career, marriage, family life, and medical questions, all are shaped by the mold of established precedent and ideal stereotypes.[6] An ecumenical approach will recognize the psychological value of tradition without allowing that value to obscure personal differences and the dynamics of modern personality. The individual matures by finding a balance between subjective needs and external models of selfhood. Neither the discipline of accepting roles inherited from the past nor the liberty of following personal impulses are absolute; both are necessary stages of the developmental process. An ecumenical approach would emphasize this process rather than one or another resolution of the dilemmas facing a modern individual.

An ecumenical approach to personal morality, then, would emphasize that ambiguity which makes choice imperative, the philosophical tension between religious values as a standard of behavior and moral worth as a function of free choice, and the psychological process of maturation which includes coming to terms with both internalized values from the past and personal promises for an independent future. This approach stands within the covenant tradition. Covenant implies personal relationship and the dynamic growth which such relationships demand. Covenant is as much a symbol of personal morality as of social loyalty. It stands for the dialectic between self and tradition just as it represents the social dialectic between public and private identity.

Two examples will help illustrate how covenantal morality can be translated into personal life. One example focuses on sexual roles and personal self-understanding. Jewish feminism raises important challenges to the Jewish woman — challenges which raise questions about Jewish values and about feminist strategy. A second illustration focuses on the question of education. Modern individuals are faced with decisions about their professional and intellectual training. How these questions are resolved entails personal as well as economic or social consequences. Personal morality must address the issue of education with as much seriousness as it addresses the question of sexual identity. These two illustrations will show how an ecumenical approach to personal morality will structure decision-making in the three spheres of Jewish self-identification, institutional responsiveness, and religious belief.

A New Personal Morality: Feminist Imaginings

An ecumenical approach listens to the various voices raised in modern Jewish discussions. Until recently these voices were predominantly male and represented a small, scholarly elite who sought answers to modern questions by investigating a literature also produced by such an elite. The contemporary discussion has introduced new voices. Men from outside the established community have interjected their opinions; women, formerly kept in silence, have begun to be heard. The unprecedented nature of their participation in this discussion is often a cause of concern. Anne Lapidus Lerner notes that tradi-

SELFHOOD AND MITZVAH

tional Jews fear Jewish feminists because they draw on non-Jewish sources. Arising from the non-traditional context, Jewish feminist voices are often listened to with skepticism.[7]

A serious Jewish consideration of women and their problems, however, may depend on listening to the views of non-Jews as well as Jews. When non-Jewish feminists add their insights to a tradition which has repressed the feminine, new moral possibilities are created. Liberation from the male domination which had characterized Judaism may require just such an external challenge. Certainly when a book devoted to "the Jewish woman" uses non-Jewish feminists to deepen and expand its horizons Judaism as a whole has benefited.[8]

One major insight contributed is that Western culture as a whole, and not merely Judaism, has confused an exploitative, male-controlled tradition with a divine fiat. Rosemary Ruether's insight that male sexual mythology is "an unnatural creation" used to repress women can be applied fruitfully to Jewish experience.[9] On the basis of this critique Cynthia Ozick explores how Jewish women's spiritual, poetic, and intellectual powers have been undermined. Even when most creative women have been condemned to a secondary position in Judaism. The myth of male superiority could not be allowed to fall, and so the evidence was tampered with.[10]

Ecumenical morality must begin by teaching women to come to terms with the ambivalent value of Judaism as their own tradition. Certainly Judaism possesses many helpful insights. There are universal truths to be found in its teachings. Such helpful insights, however, should not obscure the reality of oppression and the falsification of woman's potential which Jewish politics often produced.

Jewish feminism must be strong enough to reject the male ideology of Jewish life without rejecting other ethical insights Judaism possesses.

Women and Jewish Institutions

One temptation, of course, is to reject Jewish tradition entirely in the name of feminist truth. The challenge of traditional Judaism, however, cannot be met so easily. When one traditional spokesman declares that "The highest ideal to which a human being can aspire is to dedicate his life completely to the service of God," few can quarrel. Human beings need ideals which stimulate their development. Often an external goad is needed to prod a person to self-actualization. Judaism can provide such goads. Yet when the traditionalist goes on to explain that men fulfill this "highest ideal" by "complete and total involvement in the learning of Torah" while women do so by "the creation of Jewish hope," questions can be raised.[11] Perhaps the personal goals Judaism espouses are not to blame for its male orientation. The religious ideals of Judaism may point to true human self-realization. The institutional concretization of those goals, however, may be the source of problems. Institutionalization may pervert lofty ideals.

The institutional divisions between men and women are based on certain assumptions about human nature and the self. Even some modern rabbis and psychologists supported Jewish restrictions on women by reference to a fixed biological and psychological "nature." Woman was portrayed as either temptress or housewife, functionally designed for reproduction, psychologically symbolizing seduction. Men were imagined as the tempted, biologically created to serve culture rather than nature. This attempt at gender classification stimulated a powerful protest and initiated ongoing discussion on the subject.[12]

An ecumenical affirmation of open institutions might enable a more positive Jewish response to this challenge. Naomi Goldenberg may be right to claim that when Jewish and Christian women gain full self-consciousness they will transform their religious structures. If the ecumenical perspective is a correct interpretation of Judaism, however, she is not right to see this as the end of Judaism.[13] Certainly Jewish thinkers have pointed out how the question of women has altered many traditional forms and practices in the past. Judaism has been responsive to human need and has transformed its institutions accordingly.[14]

An ecumenical approach would argue against an inflexible view of Jewish institutions. Seymour Siegel argues that women have rights, but that congregations do as well. There must be a give and take within Jewish institutions. He suggests a flexible model. Some congregations should integrate women into their services and practices and some may retain more traditional modes. Institutions should reflect their membership. Variety rather than uniformity should characterize the congregational response to women's issues.[15] While Siegel restricts his suggestion to a congregational setting it can be applied to Judaism in general. The institution of the family need not follow any monolithic structure. The traditional model of extended kinship gave way in modern times to the ideal of the nuclear family developed in the early and middle twentieth century. New models reflecting new views of sexuality and personal interaction can be developed. Feminism may well prepare the way for a new plurality of institutional options within which Jews can develop their selfhood.

Women, Ritual, and Images of Judaism

The feminist movement challenges Jews to rethink their understanding of sexual roles and to expand the institutional options open to Jewish women. Changes in these spheres can be integrated into Jewish religiousness only when reflected in ritual experience. The belief system of Jewish life finds its concrete realization in the performance of holy acts. Sanctifying one's sexuality must take place within a religious setting. Merely changing the externals of Jewish thought or practice is not enough. For belief to be persuasive it must be part of the Jewish worship experience. An ecumenical perspective will recognize how ambiguous and problematic feminine experience is and will seek a ritualism to reflect that.

Traditional Jewish literature contains intimations of an imagery and ritualism appropriate for the modern woman. The Bible associates major social, religious and spiritual changes with women. The matriarch Sarah rather than her husband decided that Isaac and not Ishmael would be Abraham's heir. Hannah's piety put to shame the false religiousness of Eli, the priest of Shiloh. Josiah's reform of Judean religion was confirmed by the female prophet Hulda rather than a male functionary. Later Jewish writing confirms the dynamic quality of feminine influence. Jewish mystics symbolize the *Shekinah*, God's active agent for divinity in the world, as an alluring woman. Jewish women today can reclaim the revolutionary power of feminine images in Judaism and mold them into expressions of a modern woman's consciousness.

Some men are wary of this burst of creativity. David Novak urges that traditional insight provide precedent for contemporary innovation.[16] Women, however, have moved

SELFHOOD AND MITZVAH

beyond mere precedent. While ancient customs like the celebration of the new moon are revived, new rituals are invented. Traditional forms of worship, male-dominated rituals like the Passover seder and the reading from the Torah Scroll have been taken from the exclusive hold of men and revised to reflect feminine realities. Beyond this reclamation of Jewish tradition women have created wholly original rituals symbolizing birth, maturation, and personal purity. These new rituals demonstrate new options in human self-development and point to a new religious reality.[17]

An ecumenical approach to feminine morality must insist upon a positive correlation between religious language and lived reality. As religious experience changes, so too the symbols expressing it must change. Belief expressed in archaic forms loses its immediacy; rituals that are negated by life itself cannot remain persuasive. An ecumenical view of femininity requires a dialogue between subjective meaning and the objective experience ritual provides. Only in the dynamic exchange between inherited symbols, rituals alive with traditional significance, and symbols drawn from contemporary discovery, bristling with the excitement of insight and adventure, does religious meaning gain its persuasiveness. Judith Plaskow sees the necessity of this dialogue, an exchange in which religion and women both undergo change. She urges women to move "through expression of anger at God to a new relation with God," at the end of which "both women and God will emerge with new names and the power of new being."[18] That goal — new being and new names — is affirmed by an ecumenical view of covenant. Judaism itself, Jewish institutions, and personal religiousness are dynamically growing. Feminism is moral when open to this dynamic growth; Judaism finds its morality in an equally accepting dynamism of interaction with modern experience.

Education as Moral Decision

Feminism raises the question of sexual roles as a concern for personal ethics. While an intimately troubling area of human life, sexuality is but one arena for personal choice. The pattern of Jewish morality stresses that the trivial decisions of daily existence are as crucial as more dramatic ones. Personal development proceeds through countless minor actions, choices about diet, clothing, career, and education. The press of modern life often decides these choices on the basis of whim or chance; the moral dimension in such everyday choosing is often neglected. Yet religious morality consists of sanctifying these daily challenges. Abraham Heschel described Judaism as "an order in which single deeds, aggregates of religious feeling, sporadic sentiments, moral episodes become parts of a complete pattern."[19] A Jewish morality must focus on these episodes of daily living as well as on the trauma of sexuality.

The questions surrounding education form one example of moral decisons facing a modern Jew. The most important moral dimension is that of purpose. Why is education a personal necessity? Does it have only a pragmatic meaning? Are there elements in learning which transcend professional goals, intellectual curiosity, or personal self-improvement? The sense of purpose informing education will help shape the curriculum chosen. Education may be technical or humanistic; it may stress traditional content or modern research; subject matter or method may be given priority. Depending upon how education is understood the very substance of learning is constructed.

While the question of curriculum is the fundamental issue of education the institutions conveying that curriculum are equally crucial. A second moral problem is that of determining which educational authority can be trusted with the task of conveying learning. In a pluralistic setting this question of institutional responsibility is an important one. Do some institutions serve specific educational needs leaving other needs to be filled by different institutions? Is an inclusive institution to be preferred —one which integrates all spheres of learning? Society needs order as well as variety. Which serves it best — a plurality of schooling systems or a unified school system?

Both curriculum and institutional setting are provided by society. The student can select a curriculum only from courses actually offered; institutional choices are determined by their availability. A third moral decision arises when a student confronts those — naturally limited — options presented by a social context. Students must wrestle with their own motivations. Pragmatic desires often mix with idealistic goals; professional aspirations are confused with a love of learning for its own sake. While both aspects of a student's motivation are defensible, morality demands a self-examination and self-understanding. A student must make the moral choice of how and why a certain course of study is justified.

Curriculum in Jewish Perspective

The ecumenical perspective suggests that no one solution to the question of curriculum is ever satisfactory. Curriculum evolves from the interplay of tradition and modernity. The most important moral principle advanced by ecumenical ethics is that process rather than static consequences represents moral worth. In education the issue, then, is less a particular curriculum than the set of presuppositions supporting it. Ecumenical ethics defines the morality of a curriculum by its ability to respond to changing realities while continuing to confront the student with traditional content. The purpose of an ecumenically oriented curriculum should be that which Maurice Friedman characterizes as a "drawing forth what you can become in response to tradition."[20]

The first requirement of such a curriculum is that it be directly related to an individual's life. The curriculum cannot be sensed as alien, merely objective and distant. Education becomes vital when it moves from abstract teachings to direct encounter with the self. Samson Raphael Hirsch drew on Jewish tradition to declare that "the knowledge with which you have enriched your mind must be applied to *yourself*; you must recognize what you know as appertaining to you..."[21] The important aspect of learning is not content but how content can be applied. The rabbis of the Talmud knew that Jewish teachings could not be mastered by rote recitation and memory. They advised "turn it this way and that way for everything is in it" (Avot 5:22). Education is a process of subjecting a specific content to scrutiny. No content is ever fully comprehended. The point of a curriculum is the inexhaustible possibilities offered by any particular subject.

A second requirement, however, is directed to the subject matter. Curriculum does have a responsibility to be creative, to reflect the changing world of daily experience. Mordecai Kaplan has noted this challenge. He remarks that the difference between the traditionalist and the modernist is that the former is content with an unchanging content. The modernist, however much respecting and honoring the subject matter inherited from the past, augments it with new content. The substance of the curriculum as well as its meaning must be altered to meet the transformed realities of life. Kaplan suggests that the modern teacher must "create the subject matter to be taught."[22]

An ecumenical approach to education must advocate dialogue within the classroom. Both traditional content and creative subject matter must meet in a curriculum which takes its moral responsibilities seriously. A curriculum which avoids the challenges of traditional claims has evaded its responsibilty. Methods of deriving new meaning from received texts are an essential part of education. A curriculum which neglects or merely polemicizes against the modern world has also shown a moral cowardice. Such a curriculum fails to take the student's experience in daily life seriously. Unable to meet the demands of creating a new subject matter such traditionalism inculcates a self-limiting learning which conflicts with actual experience.

Educational Institutions and Ecumenical Morality

The Jew in America faced a dilemma when seeking to preserve Jewish learning. On the one hand, the public schools were the best training ground for entrance into American communal life. On the other hand, Jewish teachings were inappropriate in that setting. Wrestling with this problem Jewish institutions evolved a series of educational experiments which reflected changing styles in American pedagogy.[23] Jews recognized that Americanism is best represented by American public schools and Judaism by a Jewish education shaped by Jewish life and values.[24] The question raised most often was how compatible these two types of education really were. Could a supplemental school really convey the inclusive Jewish experience which Judaism demands? Could a Jewish day school provide an Americanizing experience that would not conflict with the democratic pluralism of the United States?

Robert Gordis has suggested that the best approach is to affirm the "very fundamental role" of the public school while pursuing a "very determined and dedicted effort to strengthen" supplementary Jewish education.[25] Ecumenical ethics would applaud such an approach. When a variety of institutions combines to offer differing educational options, the entire social system benefits. Minorities contribute to cultural diversity by their distinctive culture. Certainly they have a right to cultivate that culture.

An ecumenical ethics, however, could also support the establishment of parochial educational institutions. Religious minorities should be permitted to offer their adherents a coherent and self-contained educational program. At the same time that this permission is granted as a right, some restrictions can be imposed. When an educational institution creates barriers to intergroup communication it has violated the moral purpose of education. An isolationist education has betrayed the ideals of a pluralistic society and misrepresented reality to its students. When religious education, whether in alternative day schools or in complementary classes, opens options for those involved and for those sharing this experience, it benefits society and its students. When, however, an insular and narrow institutional program separates citizens from one another it subverts social cohesiveness and fails to fulfill its moral obligations to those it serves.

An ecumenical approach demands that religious institutions evaluate their educational programs carefully. A

SELFHOOD AND MITZVAH

moral imperative falls on both public and private education — to create channels of communication which provide increased awareness of personal choice. An institution, whether pubic or private, which abuses this ecumenical mandate and manipulates the learning process for the sake of purely parochial ends has lost sight of its moral purpose.

Education and an Intuition of Reality

Perhaps one reason education can fall into propaganda or mere technical learning lies in the mixed motivations with which students approach it. The double message —that education makes one a better person and can also insure a better job — leads to confusion. The educational process, however, can be a process of self-discovery. While learning it is possible to discover the meaning of being educated. Judaism insists that learning for its own sake is an inevitable consequence of any education. The symbolic personal power of study is reaffirmed in Judaism as part of worship, daily routine, and personal development.[26] A modern morality of education depends upon this symbolic power. An individual uses education morally when it ceases to be merely a tool for increasing chances of success and takes on a value of its own.

A student insures intellectual honesty by a constant probing of motivations. Study gains moral worth when accompanied by continual self-searching. An ecumenical approach will recognize that often friends and fellow students are the best correctives for self-deception. Education must be a continual self-exposure; exposure not only to a subject matter but to the critical challenges of colleagues is the best insurance that a student's progress is more than merely intellectual. Learning can be immoral — it can close off intimacy with others, create unbridgeable gaps within families, prevent sensitivity to peers. An ecumenical understanding of religious life will be attentive to these moral dangers. An ecumenical Judaism will never allow the accumulation of knowledge to obscure the basic purpose of learning — the ability to share oneself with other people.

Another pitfall of education is the absolutization of facts. A student often feels that a particular set of data, a specific interpretation of a text, a distinctive core of facts, provides unchanging and absolute authority. A student must learn to constantly question the subject matter of education as well as the motivation for attaining it. Martin Buber has stated that "the word . . . comes again and again from heaven as something new."[27] This is true not only merely of a revealed scripture but of all knowledge. The temptation is to fix ones learning, to solidify knowledge. An ecumenical morality insists on uncertainty. No body of learning is ever finished. Changes and development must be built into the very process of acquiring learning. The morality of education depends on sensitivity to the vulnerability and tentativeness of every human claim to understanding.

An ecumenical view of education sees it as a mirror of human reality. The careful self-scrutiny of the student reflects the ambiguity of personal motivation. Education trains a person to see the duality and duplicity of the self. As Jewish tradition discovered, study is symbolic as well as concrete. Symbolically study involves that self-doubt which reveals the dark conflicts within each individual. The external world is revealed as equally complex and uncertain as the human being. Knowledge is unmasked as theory; secure postulates and presuppositons appear under examination as based on academic prejudice. The honesty demanded by the ecumenical perspective un-

SELFHOOD AND MITZVAH

covers the radical insecurity of human pretensions of understanding. The morality of the learning process depends on the clarity with which this honest self-appraisal is conveyed.

Morality and Risk

The key to the ecumenical approach — whether to feminism or to education — is risk. Personal morality depends on being willing to risk that ambiguity and self-doubt which makes choosing significant. Jewish morality is, thus, neither a set of absolute unchanging laws nor a cipher standing of individual self-realization. Rather Judaism offers a cumulative tradition as a key to unravel the elements from the past which shaped the present. It provides a motivating impulse which propels an individual towards present decisions. Jewish morality combines inherited standards with contemporary responsiveness. This combination clarifies the risks involved in making moral choices as well as the demonic potential of abdicating decision-making altogether.

The first moral imperative of this approach is that of challenging both modern and traditional stereotypes. In the name of contemporary experience, drawing on both Jewish and non-Jewish resources, inherited patterns and roles can be questioned. The standards from the past, however, have an equal right to question contemporary assumptions. Whether these assumptions concern an educational curriculum or sexual roles the moral imperative is to listen dialectically to both modernity and tradition. An individual must discover Judaism by looking both backwards to precedent and forwards to contemporary life.

The second moral imperative is addressed to institutions. They must risk pluralism and the loss of exclusive privilege. Institutions which seek to be morally responsible risk confusing their advocates and failing to satisfy their critics. The variety of institutional options which a pluralistic society demands leads to competition and rivalry. Institutions risk their own power when they fulfill the moral demand of providing new options for those they serve.

The final moral imperative demands that students accept the risks of education — risks to themselves and their sense of security. Students must risk self-criticism to keep their motivations honest. They must risk being wrong to keep alive their willingness to change. Facing both ambivalence within and uncertainty without a student risks self-assurance when taking the moral aspect of education seriously.

Maurice Friedman suggests that "Risk is implied in the very notion of personal growth and communal authenticity."[28] Ecumenical ethics takes the acknowledgment of that risk and its essential relationship to selfhood and society as the foundation stone of personal morality.

CHAPTER FIVE
SALVATION AND ECUMENICAL ETHICS

Salvation and Religious Ethics

While morality deals with specific questions of conscience ethics addresses broader issues. Why should an autonomous human being limit personal options by self-restriction to an external set of criteria? What rationale justifies a moral component in decision-making? An ethical system usually legitimates its strictures and imperatives by referring to transcendent purpose, to a vision which surpasses transient advantages. Religious morality motivates ethical reflection by identifying its purposes with God's will. Divine sanction justifies the moral imperatives of religious ethics.

Such a religious approach conceives of every individual as a divine creation. The creator has established each creature for a certain purpose; that creature's final good depends upon its actualization of the potential intended by God. As the creature pursues a life filled with expectations and obligations deriving from divine sanction it moves towards its ultimate meaning. That ultimate goal can be described as "salvation" — perfect state of being.

The heart of religious ethics is this longing for salvation. Beyond passing goods and mundane desires, salvation stands as an absolute human value. In the name of this ideal a person is urged to sacrifice superficial goods. Longing for salvation an individual learns to ignore momentary passions.

Phillip Rieff has suggested that modernity differs from traditional religion in its appraoch to salvation. The ultimate hopes and dreams of traditional individuals transcended ordinary experience. The modern person makes ordinary life itself of ultimate worth. Traditional religion envisioned transcending the passing desires of worldly passion; salvation was an escape from the trap of daily existence. Modern individuals, in contrast, seek a therapeutic adjustment to their existence; salvation is not an escape from reality but a liberation into it. Self-fulfillment depends on spontaneous response to the possibilities of the moment and not to the self-sacrifice required by an absolute ideal.[1]

Ecumenical ethics seeks a view of salvation that draws on both the longing for transcendence and the possibilities of the moment. Such an ethics suggests that in the inevitability of conflict human beings find growth, maturity, and fulfillment. Such an ethics celebrates the tension between inherited values and modern challenges which make personal adjustment difficult. The market-place pluralism of modern society provides a proving ground for human personality and is seen in ecumenical perspective as a basic instrument of human development. Salvation, the goal towards which a human being strives, can be conceived of as a *process* rather as a state of being. Salvation consists of being in motion, in growing towards new being, in moving beyond static selfhood to an ever changing dynamic personality.

The three spheres of moral choice — *Torah*, religious teachings; *Halakhah*, the cosmic dynamics of life itself; and *Mitzvah*, the specific social and personal obligations of life — are filled with risk and conflict. *Torah* emerges from the tension between various streams of human thought. *Halakhah* can be contained by neither biology and nature nor by human ingenuity alone. *Mitzvah* cannot be identified with either traditional obligations alone or with personal desire alone. In each case the key to ecumenical morality is affirming risk, seeing the positive possibilities of conflict. The ideal of salvation from an ecumenical perspective must affirm conflict and risk as the basis of human hope and purpose.

The Ecumenical Ideal in Biblical Religion

Salvation as conflict, the ecumenical ideal which stimulates human growth and development, can be found in the Hebrew Bible. One of the various terms used to describe social and personal perfection is *shalom*. No one word can adequately translate the complex meanings associated with the term. It suggests wholeness, completeness, the creative affirmation of opposites. The restricted English translation of "peace" is misleading. A better insight is that *shalom* is an expression of salvation.[2]

The complexity of *shalom* can be seen in its use as a description of God. God is the supernal model whose ability to hold opposites together in creative tension exemplifies *shalom*. God is called the "maker of *shalom*," who creates both good and evil, light and darkness, war and peace and combines them into a single reality. When a human being follows the ecumenical pattern and affirms complexity and conflict, God's inclusiveness is being imitated. Both society and the individual have the obligation to follow God's example, to contain within themselves the same creative diversity which is within the divine.

Salvation understood as *shalom* is an ecumenical ideal. It points beyond the cessation of war, beyond national success or personal achievement to the creative potential of pluralism. When national leaders in ancient Israel reduced *shalom* to an expression of narrow national interests the prophets spoke out in protest. Jeremiah rejected such a false conception and countered the nationalistic cry of *"shalom, shalom,"* with the statement, "there is no *shalom*." Unless *shalom* stands for a creative affirmation of diversity then its promise of salvation is made in vain.

Within the ancient Israel, however, prophets of different opinions coexisted. Even Jeremiah was at times unsure whether his voice or that of his opponent expressed God's will. The biblical canon is not unambiguous as the earlier discussion of its creative character makes clear. Jeremiah's view of *shalom* must be taken together with that of his enemies. Walter Breuggemann discerns two "trajectories" in the Bible which illustrate this ambiguity. One follows the path of royal and national self-interest. This trajectory insists on national unity, on loyalty to the government and on social conformity. God has promised success and prosperity to those who affirm the national future. The second trajectory is pluralistic and dynamic. The oppressed elements in Israelite society are its true religious leadership. Society grows toward *shalom* when most responsive to the needs of these outcasts and most sensitive to the minority groups within the culture.[3]

Israel's prophets were not unambiguously on the side

SALVATION AND ECUMENICAL ETHICS

of the oppressed. Two types of prophets represented biblical religion, each springing from the point of view characteristic of one of the two trajectories. Certain prophets were "peripheral" to the national body. They identified *shalom* with transcending values and ideals that were not only beyond but sometimes even in contradiction to national interest. These peripheral prophets like Jeremiah voice social discontent. They stood at the margins of society and demanded dynamic change and growth. Other prophets, however, identified with the central institutions of political life. They considered change and revolution the greatest threat to *shalom*. These "central prophets" developed an ideology of social cohesion and loyalty to official power. Religion was understood as a support for established order and national government.[4]

Despite this double tradition the biblical intention is clear. Both social continuity and the dynamic protest of social discontent are important for communal life. Prophetic ethics is neither fully supportive of established institutions nor fully critical of them. The prophets participate in a dialogue between the supporters of stable government and those articulating the needs of society's victims. The biblical ideal is an evolving social order, a social dynamism which uses inherited forms to develop more and more liberated citizens. Norman Gottwald captures this prophetic ethics in his description of Israel's formative period. He demonstrates that biblical society was characterized most by a revolutionary *approach* to politics rather than by static institutions. Finally, he concludes, biblical faith must be judged by its ability "to clarify the range and contours of exercisable freedom within the context of the unfolding social process."[5]

Looked at in this way biblical hope depends on ecumenical conversation. Only when representative leadership and sensitive representatives of the oppressed dialogue about real possibilities is *shalom* available.

Salvation and the Wilderness Motif

Salvation understood this way is a process leading to dialogue. Such a process can be disconcerting; it represents a challenge and a trial. One element in Israelite imagery emphasizes how such a challenge and trial can lead to growth and to *shalom* — the wilderness motif.[6] In Israel's official self-description the wandering in the wilderness represents an intermediary stage linking liberation from slavery to final national achievement. In some places, Deuteronomy 26 is one example, the wandering element is omitted; in other places, Joshua 24 is such a case, the wandering is but one episode in a triumphant conquest of the promised land. In still other passages the wilderness is a place of trial, judgment and testing.

The prophet Hosea weaves these various elements together into a pattern of salvation.[7] He contrasts the place — a howling, forbidding wasteland, with its meaning, an opportunity for true response to God. Both images are appropriate and interrelated. The wilderness as a time of trial strips Israel of false pride. Naked, ashamed, and vulnerable, Israel must turn to God. At the same time as it is vulnerable, Israel is transformed. Turning to God, God returns to Israel. God and humanity discover a mutual need. The wilderness reveals how barren human institutions can be without responsiveness to changing divine demands. The divine word given in the wilderness assures humanity of God's desire for human institutions.

Hosea's distinctive message is that Israel's salvation

SALVATION AND ECUMENICAL ETHICS

depends upon its dynamic ability to expose itself to danger and to the risk of change. *Shalom* in this perspective is less the reassuring and soporific chanting of the priests, the sacrificial service of the royal court and its aristocratic power. The structures of society were mere trappings. Keeping them in place did not ensure *shalom*. Revolutionary self-exposure, however, is not enough by itself. New institutions will grow up in the wilderness. Israel's experience will lead to new ritual, new leadership, new names and new relationship. The wilderness breeds *shalom* because it provides an environment for developing new structures, new organizations, and new patterns of social life.

Traditionally the wilderness is the place of revelation. On this account revelation is but the initiation of a process. God's entrance into human life does not *settle* social issues but stimulates continual growth. Martin Buber seems to echo the wildernes motif in his view of the relationship between revelation and salvation. He too seems to see revelation as a starting point, an original impetus. Buber suggests that God calls to the creature who, on turning to God, receives a message of divine grace. That grace is not yet actualized salvation. Salvation occurs when a great unity of being emerges from a shared experience of grace which establishes "amidst all the undiminished multiplicity and manifoldness the communion of the creatures."[8] The contribution of the wilderness experience is that "communion of the creatures" based on shared exposure to divine demands. As dynamic dialogue salvation marks a beginning of interhuman relationship, not a finalized institutional structure.

Shalom and the Possibility of Ethics

The creative tension between established power and

oppressed minorities found in biblical religion, for example, the positive stimulation of the wilderness experience found in prophets like Hosea, demonstrates the possibilities for a modern ethics. That ethics will respond to the two major moral challenges of contemporary life — dogmatism and subjective self-indulgence. Dogmatic assertion that one set of rules, when explicitly and incontrovertably established provides salvation, and renders ethical decisions irrelevant. A community's absolute power obviates the possibility of choice. Moral questions are reduced to issues of facts — Is a certain act included or excluded in the religious code?

Such an authoritarian approach is attractive, but sensitivity to the real oppression and self-deception present in established power can mitigate that attraction. Biblical images suggest that no institution can be trusted to provide absolute guidance. The wilderness motif suggests that only when institutions are challenged to their deepest and most precious preconceptions can their religious potential be actualized. The wilderness demand for self-exposure will make religious men and women skeptical about absolute institutions.

A second threat to the seriousness of ethical decision-making comes from a self-oriented liberalism. Subjective values seem to preclude obedience to external guidance. Ethics is irrelevant because only the self can measure its own authenticity. The prophetic demand includes skepticism about the self, no less than about institutions. The wilderness is a place in which institutions are reborn as well as a place in which they are challenged. Individual responsibility requires the structure of institutions as well as institutional responsiveness. Ethics is essential as a means of self-discipline, and as a confession of the limitations of the self.

SALVATION AND ECUMENICAL ETHICS

Not only Jews but other American religious communities face the dilemmas of contemporary life — the problems of authoritarian ethics and the crisis of personal decisions. The ecumenical ideal of salvation as conflict, of *shalom* as the positive affirmation of contradictory aspects of human experience, offers a new type of ethical framework for moral decisions. In this new context morality depends upon listening to diverse theologies, granting the legitimacy of competing loyalties, and valuing complex religious response. Such an ethics would enable individuals to challenge their own institutions in the name of lessons learned from alternative ones. It would also impress on individuals their own vulnerability and need for external guidance. *Shalom* would transcend either purely personal self-liberation or socially conditioned reconciliation with established structures. As a productive interaction of various social forces and conflicting personal motivations *shalom* provides an ideal of salvation that makes ethical choice a practical reality in modern life.

Conclusions

The ecumenical approach to Jewish ethics contends that a religious ethics is legitimated when it responds to the concrete realities of human experience. An ethics must engage itself in life's conflicts rather than seek escape from them. This ecumenical ethics takes seriously the common problems a secular culture poses for both Jews and non-Jews. Such an ethics emphasizes three stages of moral reflection. The first is reflection on the religious tradition itself — in Judaism that entails a critical look at *Torah* from the vantage points of both tradition and contemporary life. The second stage looks at the overall design — the sense of pattern which a religion perceives in reality. For the Jew this means looking at the idea of *Halakhah* with an eye trained by modern insights into biology and science. Finally, a modern ethics must re-evaluate human deeds — both social and personal — seeing them in the context of a changing social and individual reality threatened by both dogmatism and subjective self-indulgence. Motivating the three-fold investigation is the vision of *shalom*, a dynamic affirmation of the diverse elements in human life.

How does the first reflection on religious tradition develop? Modern men and women discover new meanings in their traditions by wrestling with the challenges of modern life. Both canon as authority and Bible as inspiration for new insight are essential for an ecumenical community. Joining with other traditions which share some beliefs but challenge others religious believers are able to retain their distinctiveness and still transcend parochialism. Reflection begins when the double identity of every modern person is understood — we are both uniquely heirs of our own traditions and deeply part of a secular community.

Reflecting upon the order of the cosmos the modern individual will recognize the double responsibilty of human deeds. The natural order, a combination of inanimate and biological forces, has an integrity of its own which should not be violated. Yet human knowledge has an inner drive productive in its unique way which cannot be denied. A modern morality will stimulate dialogue between both natural order and human creativity without forcing a closed decision between the two. Religious ethics is plausible if it develops open exchange between established principles and modern possibilities of change.

Responsible action is as difficult to define as to achieve.

Temptations beset the human path — temptations to abdicate choice and allow authority to solve all problems and temptations to resist all order and external constraint. A modern ethics will point to the dangerous parochialism and self-deception possible in either option. Balanced dialogue with others and within the self can help bring a more cautious decision about either social or personal action. How social responsibility is understood must reflect the crisis of human trust precipitated by Auschwitz, Hiroshima, and Viet Nam. Personal morality can become pertinent only if the ambiguity within each soul is acknowledged. Ecumenical sharing among differing religious men and women can help demonstrate this ambiguity.

An ecumenical ethics asks religious women and men to acknowledge their own ambiguity, to confess the conflicts that tear at their social and private lives. This ethics claims that morality depends on affirming the tension which makes moral choice imperative. The prime moral imperative is a resolute refusal to escape ambivalence by retreating to a set of absolute truths which make decision unnecessary. Not everyone who seeks religious guidance will find the insecurity of an ecumenical ethics acceptable. Some, however, will respond to an ethics which listens to the symphony of varied voices in modern religious life. These people will find the differing facets of religious insight represented by dialogue liberating and challenging. They wil reject the uniformity of either traditional or subjective ethics and seek instead an open sharing of those conflicts which make moral choice a modern essential. The ecumenical ethics sketched here is an opening invitation to continued dialogue.

FOOTNOTES

Preface

1. See Eliezer Berkovits, *Faith After the Holocaust* (New York: Ktav, 1973); Eugene B. Borowitz, *How Can a Jew Speak of Faith Today* (Philadelphia: Westminster Press, 1969); *idem., The Masks Jews Wear: The Self-Deceptions of American Jews* (Port Washington, New York: Sh'ma, 1980); *idem,. Reform Judaism Today: Volume I, Reform in the Process of Change: Volume II: What We Believe; Volume III: How We Live* (New York: Behrman House, 1978, 1977, 1978); Arthur A. Cohen, *The Tremendum: A Theological Interpretation of the Holocaust,* foreword by David Tracy (New York: Crossroad, 1981); Emil L. Fackenheim, *The Jewish Return into History: Reflections in the Age of Auschwitz and a New Jerusalem* (New York: Schocken, 1978); Richard L. Rubenstein *After Auschwitz: Radical Theology and Contemporary Judaism* (New York: Bobbs-Merrill, 1966).

2. See Manachem Marc Kellner, "The Structure of Jewish Ethics," in *Contemporary Jewish Ethics,* edited by *idem.* (New York: Sanhedrin Press, 1978) 3-18.

3. Eugene B. Borowitz, "What Knowledge Does Judaism Think it Possesses?" In *Biblical Studies in Contemporary Thought,* edited by Miriam Ward (Burlington: Trinity Biblical College Institute, 1975) p. 54.

4. See the diversity in such collections as Kellner, *Contemporary Jewish Ethics;* Marvin Fox, editor, *Modern Jewish Ethics: Theory and Practice* (Athens, Ohio: Ohio State

University Press, 1975); Daniel Jeremy Silver, editor, *Judaism and Ethics* (New York: Ktav, 1970). A good summary of divergent views among Reform, Orthodox, and Conservative Jews is found in Alex J. Goldman, *Judaism Confronts Contemporary Issues* (New York: Shengold, 1978).

5. See Roland B. Gittlesohn, *The Modern Meaning of Judaism* (Cleveland, Ohio: William Collins and Wld Publishing, 19787); Bernard Martin, editor, *Contemporary Reform Jewish Thought* (Chicago: Quandrangle, 1968) and Silver, *Judaism and Ethics*; a good resource is Simeon J. Maslin, editor *Gates of Mitzvah: A Guide to the Jewish Life Cycle* (New York: Central Conference of American Rabbis, 1979).

6. See Eliezer Berkovits, *God, Man and History: A Jewish Interpretation* (New York: Jonathan David); *idem.*, *Major Themes in Modern Philosophies of Judaism* (New York; Ktav, 1974); J. David Bleich, *Contemporary Halakhic Problems* (New York: Ktav, 1977); J. David Bleich and Fred Rosner, *Jewish Bioethics* (New York: Sanhedrin Press, 1979); Immanuel Jakobovits, *Jewish Medical Ethics* (New York: Bloch, 1959); Sol Roth, *The Jewish Idea of Community* (New York: Yeshiva University Press, 1977); Moshe Halevi Spiro, *Judaism and Psychology: Halakhic Perspectives* (New York: Ktav, 1980).

7. Jacob Bernard Agus, *Dialogue and Tradition* (New York: Abelard-Schuman, 1971); Robert Gordis, *The Root and the Branch: Judaism and the Free Society* (Chicago: University of Chicago Press, 1962; *idem.*, *Understanding Conservative Judaism*, edited by Max Gelb (New York: The Rabbinical Assembly, 19787); Simon Greenberg, *The Ethical in the Jewish and American Heritage* (New York; Jewish Theological Seminary of America, 1977); Isaac Klein, *Responsa and Halakhic Studies* (New York: Ktav, 1975); *idem.*, *A Guide to Jewish Religous Practice* (New York: Jewish Theological Seminary of America, 1979); David Novak, *Law and Theology in Judaism*, foreword by Louis Finkelstein (New York: Ktav, 1974); *idem.*, *Law and Theology in Judaism*, Second Series (New York: Ktav, 1976); Sey-

mour Siegel with Elliot Gertel, editors, *Conservative Judaism and the Law* (New York: The Rabbinical Assembly, 1977).

Chapter One

1. Louis Wirth, *On Cities and Social Life: Selected Papers*, edited with an introduction by Albert J. Reiss, Jr. (Chicago: Chicago Univeristy Press, 1964), pp. 166-168; 219.

2. Jonathan Z. Smith, "Sacred Persistence: Towards a Redescription of Canon." In *Approaches to Ancient Judaism: Theory and Practice*, edited by William Scott Green (Missoula, Montana: Scholar's Press, 1978) 11-20.

3. For background see Hans Walter Wolff, "The Kerygma of the Deuteronomic Historical Work," *The Vitality of Old Testament Traditions*, edited by Walter Brueggemann and Hans Walter Wolff (Atlanta: John Knox Press, 1975) 83-100; J.M. Meyers, *The World of the Restoration* (Englewood Cliffs, New Jersey: Prentice Hall, 1968); *Traditions in Transformation: Turning Points in Biblical Faith*, edited by Baruch Halpern and Jon D. Levenson (Winona Lake, Indiana: Eisenbrauns, 1981); Robert Polzin, "Reporting Speech in the Book of Deuteronomy," 193-211; Richard Elliott Friedman, "From Egypt to Egypt: Dtr^1 and Dtr^2," 167-192; Jon D. Levenson, "From Temple to Synagogue: I Kings 8," 143-166.

4. Levenson, *Ibid.*, p. 165.

5. See Morton Smith, *Palestinian Parties and Politics that Shaped the Old Testament* (New York: Columbia University Press, 1971).

6. *Timeless Torah: An Anthology of the Writings of Rabbi Samson Raphael Hirsch*, edited by Jacob Breuer (New York: Philip Feldheim, 1957) p. 111.

7. *Ibid.*, pp. 499-505.

8. Martin Buber, *Israel and the World: Essays in a Time of Crisis* (New York: Schocken, 1963) p. 89.

9. Martin Buber, *Gleanings: A Believing Humanism*, translated with an introduction and explanatory comments by Maurice Friedman (New York: Simon and Schuster, 1967) p. 114.

10. Joseph Blenkinsopp, *Prophecy and Canon: A Contribution to the Study of Jewish Origins* (Notre Dame: University of Notre Dame Press, 1977) pp. 151-152.

11. Gershom G. Scholem, *On the Kabbalah and Its Symbolism* (New York: Schocken, 1965) p. 76.

12. *Ibid.*, pp. 61-62.

13. See James Barr, *The Scope and Authority of the Bible* (Philadelphia: Westminister Press, 1980).

14. Monika K. Hellwig, "Biblical Interpretation: Has Anything Changed?" In *Biblical Studies: Meeting Ground of Jews and Christians*, edited by Lawrence Boadt, Helga Croner, Leon Klenicki, Studies in Judaism and Christianity (New York: Paulist Press, 1980) p. 176.

15. John Bright, *The Authority of the Old Testament* (Nashville: Abingdon, 1967) p. 159.

16. Clemens Thoma refers to both Jewish and Christian institutions this way in *A Christian Theology of Judaism*, translated by Helga Croner. Studies in Judaism and Christianity (New York: Paulist Press, 1980) pp. 173-176.

17. John T. Pawlikowski, *What are They Saying About Christian-Jewish Relations?* (New York: Paulist Press, 1980) p. 65.

18. Will Herberg, *Judaism and Modern Man: An Interpretation of Jewish Religion* (New York: Harper and Row, 1965) p. 252.

Chapter Two

1. Hans Jonas, *Philosophical Essays: From Ancient Creed to Technological Man* (Englewood Cliffs, New Jersey: Prentice-Hall, 1974) pp. 8-11.

2. *Ibid.*, p. 120.

FOOTNOTES

3. Immanuel Jakobovits, "Medical Experimentation on Humans," In *Jewish Bioethics*, edited by Bleich and Rosner, pp. 378-379.

4. Norman Lamm, *Faith and Doubt* (New York: Ktav, 1971) pp. 165-181.

5. See Kellner, *Principles of Faith*, pp. 34-36, 147-147, 192-193. See also Harry Wofson, "Hallevi and Maimonides on Design, Chance and Necessity," *PAAJR XI (1941) 105-163; idem.,*"The Platonic, Aristotelian and Stoic Theories of Creation in Hallevi and Maimonides," Harry Austryn Wolfson, *Studies in the History of Philosophy and Religion I*, edited by Isadore Twersky and George H. Williams (Cambridge, Massachusetts: Harvard University Press, 1979) 234-249.

6. Wolfson, *Ibid.* Berkovits, *God, Man and History*, pp. 57-74; Jacobs, *Jewish Theology*, pp. 93-113; Lamm, *Faith and Doubt*, pp. 83-99.

7. Jacobs, *Ibid.*, p. 9.

8. Bleich, *Contemporary Halkhic Problems*, pp. 33-38.

9. Buber, *Israel and the World*, p. 180.

10. Goldman, *Judaism Confronts Contemporary Issues*, pp. 151-157; Kellner, *Contemporary Jewish Ethics*, pp. 211-237, 284-295; Bleich and Rosner, *Jewish Bioethics*, pp. 351-386, 401-450.

11. Goldman, *Ibid.*, pp. 34-62, 74-86, 109-150, 192-210, 238-246; Kellner, *Ibid.*, pp. 255-283; Bleich and Rosner, *Ibid.*, pp. 59-289; Spiro, *Judaism and Psychology*, pp. 153-167.

12. See Bleich, *Contemporary Halakhic Problems*, pp. 109-115, 325-371; Goldman, *Judaism Confronts Contemporary Issues*, pp. 35-62; and in Bleich and Rosner, *Jewish Bioethics*, Immanuel Jakobovits, "Jewish Views on Abortion," pp. 118-133; J.D. Bleich, "Abortion in Halakhic Literature," pp. 134-177; Fred Rosner, "Tay-Sachs Disease: To Screen or not to Screen," pp. 178-190.

13. Bleich, *Contemporary Halakhic Problems*, p. 340.

14. Isaac Klein, "Abortion and Jewish Tradition," *Contemporary Jewish Ethics*, pp. 270-283; Novak, *Law and Theology in Judaism*, first series, pp. 114-124.

15. Novak, *Ibid.*, p. 123.

16. Blu Greenberg, "Judaism and Feminism," Elizabeth Kolton, editor, *The Jewish Woman: A New Perspective* (New York: Schocken, 1976) pp. 188-189.

17. Balfour Brickner, "Judaism and Abortion," Kellner, *Contemporary Jewish Ethics*, pp. 279-283.

18. Seymour Siegel, "Fetal Experimentation: A Bias for Life," *Ibid.*, pp. 284-295.

19. *Idem.*, "Religion and Family Policy: A Jewish Perspective." In *Formation of Social Policy in the Catholic and Jewish Traditions*, edited by Eugene J. Fisher and Daniel F. Polish (Notre Dame, Indiana: Notre Dame University Press, 1980) p. 55.

20. Laura Hellner and Elizabeth Koltun, "Single and Jewish: Toward a New Definition of Completeness," In Koltun, *The Jewish Woman*, pp. 43-49.

Chapter Three

1. Leo Baeck, *The Essence of Judaism* (New York: Schocken, 1948) p. 88.

2. John K. Roth, *A Consuming Fire: Encounters with Elie Wiesel and the Holocaust* (Atlanta: John Knox Press, 1979) p. 117.

3. Richard L. Rubenstein, *The Cunning of History: The Holocaust and the American Future*, (New York: Harper and Row, 1975) p. 87, and passim.

4. Hannah Arendt, *The Jew as Pariah: Jewish Identity and Politics in the Modern Age*, edited and with an introduction by Ron H. Feldman (New York: Grove Press, 1978) pp. 125-222.

5. Borowitz, *Faith Today*, pp. 33, 36-40.

6. Borowitz, *Reform Judaism Today II*, p. 39.

FOOTNOTES

7. Borowitz, *Faith Today*, pp. 49-53.
8. *Ibid.*, pp. 53-57.
9. Berkovits, *Faith After the Holocaust*, p. 76.
10. *Ibid.*, p. 134.
11. *Ibid.*, p. 115.
12. *Ibid.*, p. 36.
13. *Ibid.*, p. 1.
14. Elliot Dorff, "The Meaning of Covenant: A Contemporalry Understanding." In *Issues in the Jewish-Christian Dialogue*, edited by Helga Croner and Leon Klenicki, Studies in Judaism and Christianity (New York: Paulist Press, 1979) pp. 38-50.
15. *Ibid.*, pp. 50-56.
16. *Ibid.*, pp. 56-61.
17. Martin Buber, *Moses: The Revelation and the Covenant* (New York: Harper and Row, 1958) pp. 187-188.
18. Samson Raphael Hirsch, *Horeb: A Philosophy of Jewish Laws and Observances,* translated by I. Grunfeld (London: Soncino Press, 1962), p. 382.
19. Borowitz, *Faith Today*, p. 74.
20. Buber, *Gleanings*, p. 115.
21. Abraham Joshua Heschel, *The Insecurity of Freedom: Essays on Human Existence* (New York: Schocken, 1972) p. 85.
22. Robert Gordis, *The Root and the Branch*, pp. 45-53.
23. Terence Des Pres, *The Survivor: An Anatomy of Life in the Death Camps* (New York: Pocket Books, 1977) p. 235.
24. Berkovits, *Faith After the Holocaust*, p. 61.
25. Dorothy F. Zeligs, "Abraham: A Study in Fatherhood," *Psychoanalysis and the Bible: A Study in Depth of Seven Leaders* (New York: Bloch, 1974) pp. 1-34.
26. Sklare, *America's Jews* (New York: Random House, 1971) p. 218.

27. *Ibid.*, pp. 219-222.

28. Waskow, *Godwrestling*, pp. 146-150.

29. Bleich, *Contemporary Halakhic Problems*, pp. 14-15.

30. See *Ibid.*, pp. 13-18; Waskow, *Godwrestling*, pp. 139-145; Michael Walzer, *Just and Unjust Wars: A Moral Argument with Historical Illustrations* (New York: Basic Books, 1977). The various articles in Fox, *Modern Jewish Ethics*, pp. 191-247 give a good perspective on Israeli attitudes towards these wars.

31. See the articles in Kellner, *Contemporary Jewish Ethics*, pp. 187-254.

32. See particularly Zvi Yaron, "Religion and Morality in Israel and in the Dispersion," in Fox, *Modern Jewish Ethics*, pp. 228-242.

33. See Everett Gendler, "War and the Jewish Tradition," Kellner, *Contemporary Jewish Ethics*, pp. 207-209.

34. Bleich, *Contemporary Halakhic Problems*, pp. 17-18.

35. See Kellner, *Contemporary Jewish Ethics*, pp. 319-320.

Chapter Four

1. Kellner, *Contemporary Jewish Ethics*, p. 5.

2. Jacob Agus, *Modern Philosphies of Judaism: A Study of Recent Jewish Philosophers of Religion* (New York: Behrman House, 1941) p. 343.

3. See Fox, *Modern Jewish Ethics*, pp. 166-173 and Emil B. Fackenheim, *Encounters Between Judaism and Modern Philosophy: A Preface to Future Jewish Thought* (New York: Basic Books, 1973) pp. 3-77.

4. Michael Meyer, "Problematics of Jewish Ethics," in Silver, *Judaism and Ethics*, p. 113.

5. Richard L. Rubenstein, *The Religious Imagination: A Study in Psychoanalysis and Jewish Theology* (Boston: Beacon Press, 1968).

FOOTNOTES

6. Spiro, *Judaism and Psychology*, pp. 11-30.

7. Anne Lapidus Lerner, "'Who has not made me a man,': The Movement for Equal Rights for Women in American Jewry," *American Jewish Yearbook 1977* Volume 77 (New York: American Jewish Committee, Philadelphia: Jewish Publication Society, 1976) pp. 3-38.

8. See *The Jewish Woman: New Perspectives*, edited by Elizabeth Koltun (New York: Schocken, 1976).

9. Rosemary Ruether, *New Woman, New Earth: Sexist Ideologies and Human Liberation*, a Crossroad Book (New York: Seabury Press, 1975), p. 10.

10. Cynthia Ozick, "Women: Notes Toward Finding the Right Question," *Forum* 35 (1979) 37-60.

11. Moses Meiselman, *Jewish Women in Jewish Law*, Library of Jewish Law and Ethics IV (New York: Ktav, 1978) pp. 26-33.

12. "Women and Change in Jewish Law: A Symposium," in *Conservative Judaism* XXIX: 3 v(1975) 36-48 and XXX: 1(1975) 21-62.

13. Naomi Goldenberg, *Changing of the Gods: Feminism and the End of Traditional Religions* (Boston: Beacon Press, 1979).

14. Robert Gordis, *Love and Sex: A Modern Jewish Perspective* (New York: Farrar, Straus and Giroux, 1978) pp. 87-88.

15. Siegel, "The Meaning of Jewish Law in Conservative Judaism." In *Conservative Judaism and Jewish Law*, edited by Siegel and Gertel, xxiv.

16. Novak, *Law and Theology II*, pp. 135-147.

17. See the following in Kolton, *The Jewish Women*; Cherie Koller Fox, "Women and Jewish Education: A New Look at Bat Mitzvah," 31-42; Arlene Agus, "This Month is For You," 84-93; Aviva Cantor Zuckoff, "Jewish Women's Haggadah," 94-102.

18. Judith Plaskow, "The Jewish Feminist: Conflict in

Identities," in *Ibid.*, p. 16.

19. Abraham Joshua Heschel, *Man is not Alone: A Philosphy of Religion* (New York: Harper and Row, 1951) p. 270.

20. Maurice Friedman, *The Hidden Human Image* (New York: Delta, 1974) p. 245.

21. Hirsch, *Horeb* I, p. 3.

22. Mordecai M. Kaplan, *Judaism Without Supernaturalism* (New York: Reconstructionist Press, 1967) pp. 14-15.

23. Lloyd P. Cartner, editor, *Jewish Education in the United States: A Documentary History* (New York: Teacher's College Press, 1969).

24. Walter I. Ackerman, "The Jewish School System in the United States." In Sidorsky, *The Future of the Jewish Community in America*, pp. 209-210.

25. Robert Gordis, "Toward a Philosophy for the Conservative Day School," *Proceedings of the Rabbinical Assembly of America* XXVI (1962) pp. 58-67.

26. Nathan Isaacs, "Study as a Mode of Worship." In Abraham Ezra Millgram, editor *Great Jewish Ideas*, B'nai B'rith Great Books Series (Washington D.C.: B'nai B'rith, 1963) pp. 121-131.

27. Martin Buber, *The Prophetic Faith* (New York: Macmillan, 1949) p. 164.

28. Friedman, *The Hidden Human Image*, p. 359.

Chapter Five

1. Philip Reiff, *The Triumph of the Therapeutic: Uses of Faith after Freud*, Harper Torchbooks (New York: Harper and Row, 1968) pp. 1-27.

2. Leon Morris, *The Apostolic Preaching of the Cross: A Study of Some New Testament Towns* (Grand Rapids, Michigan: Eerdmans, 1965) p. 242.

3. Walter Brueggemann, "Trajectories in Old Testament Literature," *Journal of Biblical Literature* 98:2 (1979) 161-185.

4. Robert R. Wilson, *Prophecy and Society in Ancient Israel* (Philadelphia: Fortress, 1980).

5. Norman K. Gottwald, *The Tribes of Yahweh: A Sociology of Liberated Israel, 1250-1050 B.C.E.* (Maryknoll, New York: Orbis, 1979) p. 708.

6. See Robert L. Cohn, "Liminality in the Wilderness," *The Shape of Sacred Space*, AAR Studies in Religion (Chico, California: Scholars Press, 1981) pp. 7-23.

7. On Hosea see James Luther Mays, *Hosea: A Commentary*, the Old Testament Library (Philadelphia: Westminister Press, 1969) and Hans Walter Wolff, *Hosea*, translated by Gary Stansell, Hermeneia (Philadelphia: Fortress Press, 1974).

8. Martin Buber, *Israel and the World*, p. 27.

SYMPOSIUM SERIES

1. Jürgen Moltman *et al.*, **Religion and Political Society**
2. James Grace, editor, **God, Sex, and the Social Project: The Glassboro Papers on Religion and Human Sexuality**
3. M. Darrol Bryant and Herbert Richardson, editors, **A Time for Consideration: A Scholarly Appraisal of the Unification Church**
4. Donald G. Jones, editor, **Private and Public Ethics: Tensions Between Conscience and Institutional Responsibility**
5. Herbert Richardson, editor, **New Religions and Mental Health: Understanding the Issues**
6. Sheila Greeve Davaney, editor, **Feminism and Process Thought: The Harvard Divinity School/Claremont Center for Process Studies Symposium Papers**
7. International Movement, A.T.D./Fourth World, **Children of Our Time: The Children of the Fourth World**
8. Jenny Hammett, **Woman's Transformations: A Psychological Theology**
9. S. Daniel Breslauer, **A New Jewish Ethics**